Ordi
Enlightenment

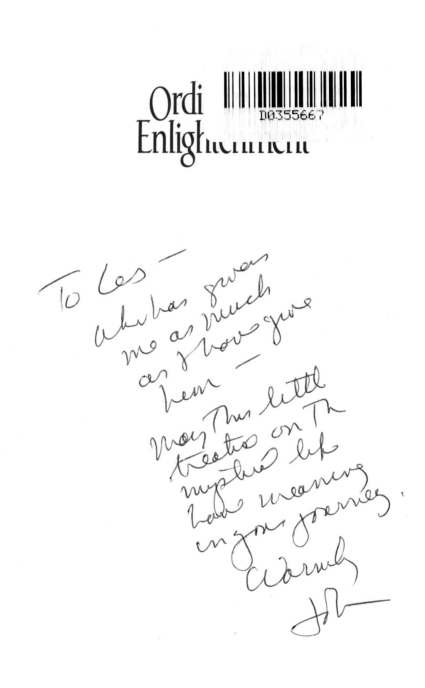

To Les —
who has given
me as much
as I have given
them —
may this little
treatise on the
mystery of life
had meaning
in your journey.
Warmly,

Also by John C. Robinson, Ph.D.:

*But Where Is God? Psychotherapy and the
Religious Search*

*Death of a Hero, Birth of the Soul:
Answering the Call of Midlife*

Ordinary Enlightenment

Experiencing
God's Presence
in Everyday Life

Unity Village, Missouri

First Edition 2000

Unity House is a publishing imprint of Unity School of Christianity. To receive a catalog of all Unity publications (books, cassettes, compact discs, and magazines) or to place an order, call the Customer Service Department: 816-969-2069 or 1-800-669-0282.

The publisher wishes to acknowledge the editorial work of Michael Maday, Raymond Teague, and Medini Longwell; the copy services of Kay Thomure, Marlene Barry, and Beth Anderson; the production help of Rozanne Devine and Jane Blackwood; and the marketing efforts of Allen Liles, Dawn O'Malley, and Sharon Sartin.

Cover design by Gretchen West

Cover photo by Adri Berger/Tony Stone Images

Interior design by Coleridge Design

Library of Congress Card Number: 99-67065

ISBN 0-87159-261-4

Canada BN 13252 9033 RT

Table of Contents

Introduction

Presence refers to the immediate and tangible experience of God's consciousness—in the world and in our own being. This book is an invitation to experience that Presence directly.

Mystics, saints, and the very devout have referred to the Presence for centuries, but few have left us with practical instructions for *experiencing* it. Maybe the process is impossible to describe. Maybe the Presence is a gift of grace that cannot be encountered intentionally. But that's not what I have found. Based on my own firsthand experiences, and those of countless others, this book will describe:

- The surprising ways Presence leaks into our everyday lives.

- That profound breakthrough of Presence, known as the mystical experience, that can happen to anyone at any time.

- Extraordinary insights about God and reality revealed in the Presence.

- The experiential qualities and dynamics of Presence.

- How to locate and experience the Presence.

- What the experience of Presence is like.

- How the world returns to Eden again in the Presence (and 21 observations from Edenic consciousness).

- The nature and experience of mystical union.

- 24 additional exercises for locating and entering the Presence.

- The ecstatic poetry of Presence.

- The way Presence transforms suffering and evil.

- How healing takes place in the Presence.

- Ordinary Enlightenment: The everyday experience of Presence.

◆ 7 keys to the Gates of Eden.

But first, let me digress. You'll see why in a moment.

Breakfast With an Old Friend

Sitting outside with Eric, an old friend, eating breakfast together on a quiet patio, sharing the headlines and stories of our lives, I began talking about my interest in the Presence.

"Have you ever sensed or felt the Presence of God?" I asked, hesitantly, remembering Eric is not a particularly religious guy.

Eric thought for a moment and then surprised me with his answer. "Yes," he said. "But it's not something big or dramatic. It's a quiet kind of feeling that comes over me when everything is relaxed and peaceful. There is a deep contentment and a sense that the world is really okay just the way it is. At such times," he added, "life feels especially precious." Exploring Eric's experience a little further, we also discovered that it was not about getting, fixing, or achieving anything. It had more to do with letting go and coming fully into the present moment.

Then, as Eric and I continued talking, something rather extraordinary happened. The experience of

Presence began to open all around us, and in its gentle ambiance, the world subtly changed.

The space in which we sat became wonderfully still, and I remarked how velvety soft the air and sunlight felt on my skin. Even the muffled traffic sounds became part of this timeless moment of spontaneously heightened and crystal-clear awareness. I realized, too, that this awareness was not so much in me, or us, but around us; or more accurately, it seemed like we were in it! And the world we were in seemed transformed in loveliness. Eric noticed that my plate, left with a few fruit rinds and jelly smears, was more beautiful than any work of art. Everything we looked at in this nonjudgmental and expanded awareness seemed brighter, more vividly colorful and distinct.

I described to Eric how my own experience of Presence always felt kind, patient, and accepting, and that whatever agitation or distress I might be feeling often dissolved in its warm and loving consciousness. Yes, Eric noticed, his earlier feelings of hurt and frustration about a personal problem had dissipated, and he felt more understanding and forgiving toward the people involved. That surprised him. Indeed, this most ordinary experience of Presence had changed us both, for we found ourselves feeling happier, moving and talking more slowly, and enjoying this quiet communion with each other, *and with the Presence.*

"Everyday worries don't matter much in this space," Eric concluded. "Or maybe it's just that everything is already perfect just as it is. Perhaps we are the problem." Contemplating this last remark, we grew silent. The world, radiant and full of Presence, was enough.

Unhurried, the sun climbed higher in the sky. Eric and I said our good-byes and parted peacefully. Amazingly, breakfast with an old friend had become an experience of Presence. It happened as simply as breathing. Was it just imagination?

It's Really Quite Common

Experiences of Presence actually occur far more frequently than we realize. Let me explain:

Quite by coincidence (or was it?), I was recently sitting in a group of people planning a spirituality center. We began to share our own experiences of holy ground, a metaphor for times when the sacred feels present, intimate, and available. Interestingly, every person in the group of fifteen or so described an experience of Presence, and I can still remember some of the ways its soft, loving energy had touched each of their lives: sitting deep in a redwood grove saturated with the living consciousness of trees, earth, and air; feeling waves of inexplicable ecstasy listening to Handel's *Messiah* on Christmas Eve; running alone on the beach until the beach, the ocean, and the running came together into one seamless whole; experiencing personal consciousness start to expand into the vast expanse of a starry night sky; holding a grandchild for the first time and marveling at the miracle of life; noticing that instant when the church choir begins to sing as one multioctave voice; sensing an awesome energy emanating from the ancient walls of a Pueblo ceremonial Kiva; sharing times of simple, loving kindness that dissolve the walls between people; and perceiving moments of unexpected wonder and awe when time, and everything else, seems to stand still, for no apparent reason.

Like the blind men touching different parts of the same elephant, each person's experience of Presence is part of a much larger mystical possibility: communion with the imminent and omnipresent Divine. Easily overlooked or discounted, these partial experiences of Presence are actually doorways to God. Let's go further. Sometimes experiences of Presence open to us in times of pain and hardship.

In Pain and Hardship

Morrie, an older friend of mine actively involved in Alcoholics Anonymous, told me that he often senses the Presence in AA groups. It is not just because of AA's spiritual orientation, he clarified. It happens when a person has the courage to share something painfully honest. Morrie described it: "The room becomes very silent—you can hear a pin drop—and I feel the Presence in the room. I think other people feel it too. We just don't name it." This experience of Presence can break through anytime a person speaks directly from the heart. I remember a famous workshop leader stepping out of his prepared remarks to describe the death of his son. The unexpected disclosure of his deep and personal sorrow created a hushed, tender, and profound aura of sacredness in the room. I believe the entire gathering felt the Presence that day holding us gently in Its love.

Crises, too, may bring us into the Presence. Can you recall a terrible or frightening situation—a sudden death, automobile accident, or natural disaster—when your everyday mental chatter ceased entirely? Time stopped. Thinking stopped. Only the now existed. It was like that when President Kennedy was assassinated or the space shuttle blew up or as the first pictures of the Oklahoma City bombing came into our living rooms. At such times, we are so completely in the present that we seem to experience (and be absorbed by) a larger consciousness—omnipresent, silent, and aware. It may not occur to us to call it the Presence of God.

We also sense the Presence in major life transitions like birth, marriage, and death. For example, the day my father died, everything seemed different. Despite my grief, his room glowed with holiness, and the hills on the drive home were intense with consciousness, pregnant with a significance I could not quite understand but bowed to nonetheless. I was literally in the Presence, floating in a consciousness that held me, well, like a father. Hardship, too, can bring with it opportunities to experience Presence. I have frequently heard people describe how literally close they felt to God during their most difficult life experiences. Indeed, any severe or prolonged physical or emotional stress (e.g., near death, high fevers, anesthesia, starvation, dehydration, sleep deprivation, profound emotional shock) can take us into the Presence, and many extreme religious practices are based on this phenomenon.

If you haven't personally had this kind of experience of Presence, ask around—you will be surprised at how often it happens.

The "Creative Zone"

When I was writing my first book, *Death of a Hero, Birth of the Soul,* there were times when it felt like *it* was writing me. Complex ideas and insights about

the male midlife passage would flow through me unabated, clarifying themselves, mixing in unexpectedly creative ways, and completely absorbing my
attention. Six or seven hours would feel like minutes,
with no awareness of hunger, noise, time, or weather.
I was in a silent bubble. Nothing existed except this
uninterrupted stream of understanding from the center of my being to the moving text on the computer
screen.

A remarkable and unplanned state of consciousness had taken over my work, a creative alchemy to
which I repeatedly surrendered without even a thought.
Individuality dissolved into a jet stream of consciousness, action, understanding, flowing directly from a
temporary unity of Being. In fact, it seemed as if "I"
were not even in the experience, replaced by a symphony of thought, key strokes, and words. It felt like
dreaming a book into existence. Afterwards I was
amazed at what I had written, learning as if for the
first time what I apparently already knew.

These intensely creative experiences reveal many
of the qualities associated with Presence: stillness,
clarity, timelessness, absorption, and wonder. Added
are two others: a complete absence of self and an effortless flow of knowledge and activity. Athletes call
this dimension of Presence the "zone" and describe
their entire competitive reality becoming a fluid yet

highly focused whole where everything they try works smoothly and effortlessly. My son says that in his heightened consciousness, he can see the threads on a 90 mph fastball: they rotate slowly, the ball appears to be the size of a grapefruit, and whenever this happens, he knocks the daylights out of it.

Some people seek this state of self-transcending consciousness through danger.

Dangerous Pursuits

I know a man who is daily crushed and exhausted by his work. A doctor in a large hospital, with patients scheduled every eight minutes, Frank finds that his psyche and soul are so deadened by the end of the day that he can hardly feel anything. On weekends, however, when the cascading Sierra rivers are full and fast, Frank heads for the white water. In its turbulence, immense power, and ever-present danger, there is no time to think. With senses wide open and acutely sharpened, with cold water striking his face, and nature bursting with beauty all around him, Frank is suddenly intensely alive—one with his oars, the river's roar, and the moment-by-moment experience of his own responding. There is no past or future. Even the concept of "present" is gone. Worry, responsibility, and self are swallowed entirely by this enormous, raw, sensory experience that always seems to heal and restore him.

I know another man who tobogganed off the 3,000-foot cliffs of El Capitan in Yosemite National Park with a parachute on his back, and another who ran the churning brown waters of the Colorado River deep in the Grand Canyon *in a wet suit*! Can you imagine the awesome power of these experiences? Why do people take such risks? Skydiving, bungee jumping, car and motorcycle racing, rock climbing—these are dangerous activities! Certainly some of the men and women in these sports are simply after excitement or self-glorification. But others will tell you about a clarity of consciousness like none other: so intensely here and now, so acutely awake and aware, with senses so fused with physical reality that they achieve a timeless, self-forgetting, joyous, and paradoxically serene experience of ultimate being.

While most daredevils would probably not call their risk-taking activities religious, think about it: You have to be "out of your mind" to do these things, and perhaps that's the point. "Mind," as mystics have told us for centuries, is a barrier to the experience of Presence, and intentional danger certainly breaks through that barrier.

But let's continue. This next experience of Presence erased mind and self completely, at least temporarily.

On Golden Pond

I recently stayed a week with two of my brothers by a lake in New Hampshire. It was October and the brilliant fall colors were everywhere—deep burgundy, bright orange, earth tones, and speckled yellows—carpeting the ground like a Persian rug, reflecting boldly off the lake, swirling in the afternoon wind, and setting trees aflame in shimmering golden light whenever the sun burst through the eastwardly rolling clouds. We were a minister, a computer programmer, and a psychologist, strolling along the deserted lake shore, bundled up in winter coats in the deepening afternoon shadows, sharing life. We came to a bench and sat for a moment, gazing on the water. An icy wind portending the approaching winter numbed the edges of our ears. The scene, like one of those photographs from an insurance calendar, was strikingly beautiful.

It happened suddenly, quietly, stealing upon us unannounced, like an ancient, long-forgotten consciousness. Its silence englobed us, and the longer we sat, the deeper it became. Our collective awareness, riveted by the wind-whipped water, darkening tree-silhouetted horizon, and bitter cold air, sharpened to crystal clarity. Was it just the silence? No, it was more. A space without words, thoughts, or even mind had swallowed our individual existences. Ten, fifteen, twenty minutes—we never really knew how long we sat there, transfixed, with no residue of individuality or time or purpose. Suspended in a pure and heightened awareness, we had disappeared into a stillness that seemed to hold all Creation, leaving only the vividly stark beauty of the glacial lake.

When "it" was over, when one brother finally shifted position, and another cleared his throat, and the spell broke, returning us to something closer to "normal" consciousness, we got up and began walking in silence, savoring what had just happened. Brothers, who customarily talk with ease, could only begin hesitantly.

"Wow . . ."

"Did something extraordinary just happen?"

"Yes! Wasn't that amazing?"

"It was incredible."

"How long were we there?"

"I don't know. It seemed like an eternity."

"Yes, as if we had slipped into a vast, empty sea of awareness."

"Totally, and the 'I' in my personality dissolved completely in that sea."

We lapsed again into silence. Words could not hold what had just happened.

How do you categorize this kind of experience?

Non-ordinary? Transcendent? Transpersonal? Even big words fail. Was it extraordinary? Certainly. Was it timeless? Yes, as if eternity had broken through time. Otherworldly yet intensely real, it felt like a "religious experience." The overused word *enlightenment* comes to mind, yet it was all so ordinary: the world we looked at every day. Ordinary enlightenment? Something like that.

Now let's take one last quantum leap into the ultimate experience of Presence. The big one.

Lifting the Veil

Jerry had no particular thought in mind when he sat down on the park bench that cold, wintry day. He was between jobs—one of hundreds of men laid off from the factory in recent months. He had taken to going for long walks between job applications and visits to the unemployment office. Then, as was his custom, Jerry stopped in the park to pass the time. There was nothing much else to do.

At first he dismissed the changing light, thinking perhaps the overcast sky had thinned enough to brighten the dismal day. The sudden stillness that enveloped the park, however, caught his attention. It was incredible. Even more interesting was the way his mind seemed to clear all by itself. Thinking ceased, replaced by an inner silence and an acutely sharpened awareness of everything. Yes, something was distinctly different. His constantly chattering mind had fallen away, and he had stepped outside of time.

Despite the overcast, the park now seemed full of light, as if lit from within, and everything he saw in that light was exquisitely beautiful. Touching a closely pruned rosebush beside the bench, Jerry was entranced by its luminous shade of green and the way the stem rolled pliantly between his fingers. He had forgotten how remarkable the world really was! He gasped at the iridescent sparkle of a dew drop on the bench, marveling at how it magnified the underlying wood grains. A birdcall pierced the silence with its sweet and brilliant clarity. Then, as if spoken by another consciousness, the thought arose, "The world is a paradise of extraordinary splendor, yet you miss it every day in your worry." It was true: there was no ugliness or imperfection here. It just didn't exist. He could not conceive of any evil, for everything he saw now felt holy.

The next thing Jerry noticed was an awareness not his own. There was indeed another consciousness in the park. It was everywhere—in the light, the surrounding space, the plants, rocks, and earth. The world had awakened and in its consciousness, everything was intensely alive, aware, and somehow filled with intelligence. Then he felt it surround him! Jerry was now held in an unconditionally loving Presence—tender, intimate, and friendly—into which he surrendered with complete and unquestioning trust.

It was, he sensed, a consciousness that transcended time, yet held and knew everything that existed in time. Briefly, merged with this Presence, it seemed to Jerry that he, too, extended through all time and space, as if he knew everything and was himself part of everything. His boundaries had disappeared. Nothing was alien, unfamiliar, remote, or separate. He was one with the rosebush, the bench, the distant bird, even the surrounding space. In fact, reality was all one living, breathing, interwoven Being. And in the Presence of this Being, every single thing was infinitely precious, peacefully cradled in an indestructible and timeless love.

Was this heaven? Heaven on Earth? Eden? Since he was infused with sacred consciousness, all he encountered now was divine, eternal, and holy. Plants, animals, people, and things, even Jerry himself, were made of the same living, radiant substance. The sheer joy he felt exceeded anything he had ever known. The world, he knew in this instant, was nothing less than the Presence and Being of God.

Overflowing with humility, gratitude, and joy, and feeling as if he were at the most sacred of altars,

Jerry actually fell to his knees and thanked God for this revelation. More than a vision, he knew unmistakably that he had been shown the actual nature of the world, that his life and all life were holy, and that there was nothing more important than knowing this. He was done, he realized, with all searching, all dogma, indeed all questions about meaning, purpose, or religion, for reality had itself become sacred, ending his search and silencing his questions. The world he lived in every day, the very place he sat, held the secret of existence, and this secret was God's immanent and always available Presence.

Jerry had no idea how long he had been in this state—how can you measure time in timelessness?—but gradually, almost imperceptibly, the Presence drained away, returning him to the "ordinary" park he had first entered. Yet even as this happened, his joy continued unabated. Jerry knew now, beyond the shadow of a doubt, that everything would be okay. However his job situation worked out, or didn't work out, mattered not at all, for he knew that this Presence, whether he felt it or not, would always be there, holding him and his family in its unconditional love. And he knew he would experience this unity again, if not during his lifetime, when he died. His fear of death was gone forever.

Jerry remained in the park for a long time after

his everyday consciousness returned, reflecting on his
experience. He had seen God, not as he had once expected, but as God really was: the world filled with
Presence. And he knew that even though his regular
problems would still be here—unemployment, overdue bills, concern for his family's well-being—*he*
would never be the same. Jerry walked home from
the park with a brand-new feeling—a trust in the universe, in life, and in God's constant, intimate, everywhere Presence.

The Purpose of This Book

From the everyday sacred to Jerry's full-blown
mystical experience, Presence is always leaking (or
breaking!) into human consciousness. These vignettes
describe "the varieties of religious experience," to
borrow William James' famous title. They describe
unexpected shifts from our customary—and heavily
clouded!—mental state into ever more pure and intense experiences of God.

But the purpose of this book is not to talk *about*
God or higher states of consciousness, for countless
volumes in the religious, psychological, and New Age
sections of bookstores and libraries do that. The purpose is to *experience* God. I want to lead you into a
remarkable kind of consciousness, one that opens di-

rectly into the Presence, overcoming the uncontrollable nature of most mystical experiences. This is not a new religion; it is the oldest of religions; it is the basis of every religion. Simply put, our native ability to experience the imminent Divine, available since the dawn of time, has been neglected, dismissed, and sometimes even forbidden in the rise of Western science and formal, hierarchical religion. This has been a tragic but entirely reversible error. Originating from firsthand mystical consciousness, *Ordinary Enlightenment* was written to help you restore your own experience of Presence. Are you interested?

Before we embark on this extraordinary journey, however, a few introductory remarks are necessary. I did not begin with this book. Many of the ideas and experiential exercises described here seemed so controversial that I wrote two previous books to lay the necessary foundation. The first, *Death of a Hero, Birth of the Soul,* describes the psychological and spiritual challenges inherent in the male midlife passage. Its surprising spiritual thesis is this: the death of the heroic quest at midlife, combined with the experience of aging, brings to the spiritually mature man an epic moment when time and the story he believes to be his life both end. With that startling realization, awareness opens (albeit briefly and subtly at first) to an Edenic consciousness originally encountered in earliest childhood, a reality pervaded by Presence. *But Where Is God? Psychotherapy and the Religious Search*, my second book, then presents a psychospiritual model outlining the progressive interaction of ego, self, soul, and the Divine that leads us back to this unity consciousness and emphasizes the importance of integrating spiritual transformation into the psychotherapeutic journey.

Ordinary Enlightenment now strives to bring mystical consciousness into the reader's immediate and personal experience. Avoiding the confusion of complex theological debate and esoteric disciplines, it goes straight to the point: There is a Presence in the world (and within us) that can be located and experienced directly. Entering the Presence, we not only confirm the remarkable revelations of Jerry's mystical experience, we also discover our own ultimate nature. Then the world and our lives are transformed in ways we could never imagine. And the proof I wish to offer for these wild assertions is your own experience.

The argument developed in this book is not new. Historically it would be labeled *pantheism* (*pan-theism*: everything=God), the belief that God and the world are one and that everything in the world, indeed the world itself, is divine.

Though often the minority voice, proponents of

pantheism have appeared in nearly every religion, usually from within its mystical wing, and emerge anew with every generation and religious movement. Not surprisingly, it has as many faces as the religions and philosophies spawning it (e.g., Brahmanism, Stoicism, Neoplatonism, Gnosticism, Monism, Sufism, Mystical Christianity). A sampling of notable historical figures inclined toward pantheism includes Heraclitus, Plotinus, Eckhart, Ign Al'Arabi, Chuang Tzu, Zeno of Citium, Scotus, Spinoza, Bruno, Aquinas, Boehme, Toland, Rousseau, and Hegel.

Like any other religious or philosophical orientation, pantheism also hosts its own divisions and controversies. In the Judeo-Christian tradition, for example, the emphasis on God's transcendence and the goal of reaching heaven sometime in the future makes pantheism unacceptable. In fact, the Catholic Church has repeatedly condemned pantheism, sometimes even equating it with atheism. *Panentheism*, the belief that God is present and sensible in the universe but also transcends it, allowed other Christian writers to flirt with the idea without incurring disapproval from their superiors. Another position, scientific pantheism, views the verifiable laws of the universe as equivalent to God's mind.

As the reader will readily see, the pantheistic thread running throughout *Ordinary Enlightenment* is largely based on collections of mystical experiences and my own mystical phenomenology. Again, it encourages each person to test and confirm its tenets through personal, firsthand experience.

Finally, the material in this book represents a spiritual confession—a window into my own transformation, shared not as proof for any personal superiority but as an entirely commonplace example of the mystical consciousness available to each of us. A lifetime of reading, discussing, following the mystical path, and looking deeply into the waters of consciousness gradually allowed me to understand the essential message of mystics across the ages. Moreover, this work is also the legacy of a well-trained and seasoned mental health professional—a clinical psychologist with over twenty-five years of experience who is no longer seduced by spiritual fads and fancies. I write instead from an experienced mysticism, one that reveals God to be real, alive, present, and knowable. You have that same capacity.

Invitation

This book is about learning to experience the Presence—here, now, literally, directly—and discovering how mystical consciousness can transform your life. It can make a huge difference in how you experience your life—your level of happiness, your health, your prosperity. It doesn't matter what religion you practice or don't practice, or what you believe or don't believe. You are invited to come with me deep into the Presence of the universe and find out for yourself what the mystical realization of God is all about. You will find extraordinary spiritual propositions, practical explanations, powerful transformational exercises, ecstatic poetry, a surprising analysis of suffering and evil, and guidelines for living in a world saturated with Presence. Join me; I'll show you what I've seen.

But wait. Do these promises strike you as ridiculous, outrageous, or even heretical? Good, I have your attention! This book is about the actual mechanics of enlightenment, challenging you to overthrow all you "think" you know for contact with the living divine universe. But I need you to be fully awake, alert, and present. Read this book slowly, carefully, consciously, over and over. Discover, test, and prove each proposition for yourself, until you are fully ready to leave all ideas for the actual experience of God. May your journey into the Presence be rewarding, powerful, and transformative.

Chapter One

Preparation

The cosmos, which to the self conscious mind seems made up of dead matter, is in fact far otherwise—is in very truth a living presence.[1]

—Richard Bucke

This "sense of God" is not a metaphor. Innumerable declarations prove it to be a consciousness as sharp as that which other men have, or think they have, of colour, heat, or light. . . . Such a sense of the divine presence may go side by side with the daily life and normal mental activities of its possessor; who is not necessarily an ecstatic or an abstracted visionary, remote from the work of the world.[2]

—Evelyn Underhill

HAVE YOU EVER HAD an experience like those described in the Introduction? I believe they happen (or begin to happen) to everybody, though we may suppress, dismiss, or forget them. In fact, Abraham

Maslow found that with careful questioning nearly everyone he interviewed could recall moments of heightened mystical awareness he labeled "Peak Experiences." These breakthroughs of expanded consciousness are not evidence of insanity or rabid imagination. Rather, they are times when the world suddenly becomes transparent to the Presence, when the mystical dimension temporarily fills and transforms our awareness. But Presence is actually a spiritual reality that surrounds us all the time. As William Blake described, "If the doors of perception were cleansed every thing would appear to man as it is, infinite."[3]

What would we see if the lens of perception were cleansed? Definitely not what we *think*! In this chapter, I want to challenge, even shatter, our everyday assumptions about God and reality with some radical revelations about spiritual life taken directly from the mystical experience. Consider this a preparation for your own experience of Presence. If you keep an open mind, these ideas should intrigue, excite, and astound you. But first we need to establish our basic spiritual vocabulary and then deepen our understanding of two key processes: mystical consciousness and mystical experience.

Basic Vocabulary

In the religious domain, definitions are often controversial. Some words change their meaning over time. For example, the distinction between *religion* and *spirituality* is a fairly recent one and disagreement continues over its legitimacy. Other words such as *God*, *Presence*, and *Being* have been defined in different ways by theologians and philosophers over the years, leading to complex and sophisticated debate. The definitions presented here, however, are not meant to be controversial or to conform precisely to any particular tradition (though they certainly overlap with most). Their purpose is to establish a common frame of reference for our discussion of the sacred and to help you discover for yourself the *experiences these terms point to*.

Presence, as you recall, refers to the immediate and tangible experience of God's consciousness in the world and within our own being.

Being refers to God's physical manifestation in the world and is recognized when "things" (animate and inanimate) are experienced as actual forms of the Divine.

Mysticism is that branch of religion which deals with the direct, immediate, and firsthand experience of God, in contrast to the secondhand knowledge contained in scripture, theology, and philosophy. All the experiences of Presence described in the Introduction would fall under the general category of mysticism.

Mystical Consciousness is our natural (though underused) ability to tune in to the mystical dimension of the world, allowing us to intentionally recognize and experience the Presence and Being of God. While it may seem unusual to claim so, it is a skill that can increase with understanding and practice.

Mystical Experience, on the other hand, refers to those remarkable moments, unexpected and beyond our control, in which the Divine literally and profoundly infuses and transfigures the world with its Presence and Being. Mystical experiences can be further divided into *major* (i.e., full-blown), *minor* (i.e., partial), and *borderline* (right-on-the-edge) categories.

By these criteria, "Breakfast With an Old Friend" is an example of mystical consciousness, for our awareness of the Presence opened as a result of the way we intentionally focused on its experiential qualities. "Lifting the Veil," of course, would be an example of a major mystical experience, for it was unexpected, involuntary, and profound. All the remaining examples of Presence ("It's Really Quite Common," "In Pain and Hardship," "The Creative Zone," "Dangerous Pursuits," and "On Golden Pond") would represent minor mystical experiences. The borderline variety happens when we come right up to a mystical experience (e.g., suddenly the world begins to be remarkably beautiful, luminous, and beyond time) but can go no further, and it dissolves quickly. By now it should be evident that moments of Presence and Being happen far more often than we realize.

Because mystical consciousness and mystical experience are so central to the experiential goals of this book, we need to describe their nature and dynamics in more detail.

More on Mystical Consciousness

I have known mystical consciousness since early childhood. It's an awareness I discovered quite naturally, probably by dint of temperament and interest, and now find myself drawn to more and more frequently as my spiritual life unfolds. Only recently, however, have I attempted to understand and describe it objectively to teach others. What does mystical consciousness entail? Is it really a natural ability? And why isn't it more commonly used and appreciated? Though the following discussion may seem a little academic at first, don't be put off; you will soon see just how important this process really is.

As the actual words imply, there are two parts to this skill: a certain kind of *consciousness*, and that experiential dimension of the world we call *mystical*. Let's examine each part further.

The consciousness I am describing involves an especially pure form of awareness, one that is:

- Intentionally heightened and sharply focused.

- Free of the usual contents and contaminants of consciousness (e.g., thought, memory, imagination, fantasy, emotion, expectations, and attitudes).

- Highly sensory.

- Acutely here and now.

This lucid, highly alert, noncognitive awareness is often used instinctively to locate an unidentified danger in the world (e.g., the way people or animals suddenly stand very still, keenly focusing awareness into the environment in search of an unseen presence). As a result, it is exceptionally well suited for sensing *the* Presence, and soon I will show you how. This same consciousness can also be focused on everyday physical reality, but in a very nonordinary way, for it involves seeing the world exactly as it is, unfiltered by labels, expectations, or thoughts of any kind. Mystical consciousness involves this kind of pure and naked perception, completely released from the tyranny of the conceptual mind. It should be apparent that such clarified consciousness is an ability we all have but use only infrequently.

The word *mystical* implies that what we are tuning in to is the Divine, which manifests as both Presence and Being. Sensing the Presence involves focusing this heightened, crystal-clear awareness into the unseen but omnipresent consciousness of God. Being, the physical dimension of the Divine, is discovered when the world itself is perceived with this same intense clarity. Our own body, of course, is part of that Being, and its divine ground can be directly experienced by focusing this purified awareness on feelings in the body. Ultimately, of course, Presence and Being are one, an equivalence verified in major mystical consciousness. Don't be daunted by this explanation, and remember that these terms will make more sense as we begin to apply them. Now let's turn to the mystical experience.

A Deeper Look at the Mystical Experience

One of the great driving forces in my life has been to experience God directly. The experience goes by countless names: *satori*, enlightenment, *nirvana*, Christ consciousness, Holy Spirit, *kundalini*. I didn't want intellectual beliefs, somebody else's version of the ultimate, or even a beautiful fantasy; I wanted God.

Nearly every religion—or at least its mystical branch—implies that direct and firsthand experience of Ultimate Reality is possible. After all, each founder of the various religions likely had one, and the scriptures and practices that followed generally suggest that others could too. In fact, ecstatic encounters with the Divine are described by famous saints and mystics in virtually all traditions, but how does the average person replicate these glorious and sublime experiences?

Over the years I read widely in the world's religious literature, finding many wonderful and encouraging nuggets of information on the experience of the Divine. But a lot of what I read was also confusing, irrelevant, and even contradictory, perhaps because I was "outside" the particular religion and its specialized vocabulary; perhaps because it was presented by teachers or followers who had never personally experienced the founder's original vision; or, perhaps as the history of every religion demonstrates, power, politics, and personality can and do distort our understanding of the mystical life. And, as a Buddhist friend recently pointed out to me, much of religion is intended to promote "faith, devotion, good works, and ethical living," not the direct experience of God.

Nevertheless I kept searching. As a skeptical psychologist, I was drawn especially to empirical accounts of sacred experience and avidly followed the near-death literature from its inception. I interviewed people who reported leaving their bodies in acute medical emergencies and crossing over into a spiritual dimension where they encountered deceased loved ones, beautiful landscapes, and a Divine Being. Deathbed visions held a similar interest for me, and I especially recall those described by my father and grandmother. I came to realize that these experiences, while profoundly important, generally say more about the purpose of life and what happens after death than what it means to experience God here and now. All the while I continued to explore most of the well-known practices and pathways to religious experience found throughout the world (e.g., prayer, meditation, contemplation, teachers, drugs, vision quests), trying to understand what really constitutes a "religious experience" and how it happens.

Then, several years ago, I read my first description of the full-blown mystical experience, the kind that happens not just to famous saints or gurus, but to everyday people like Jerry. And like Jerry on the park bench, I was startled. This, I knew, was IT. Here was an undeniable firsthand experience of God's Presence and Being in the world, as the world, and as the ultimate nature of existence.

Seized with an urgent need to review more cases, I soon discovered a nearly endless supply of examples in the literature, amongst my friends and patients, even in my own life—in fact, all around me. Surprisingly, most mystical experiences occurred unexpectedly to people who were not actively seeking them. Many were not even religious. But all knew without any doubt that they had experienced God directly, though not the way any had been led to expect. When I abstracted the remarkable teachings of the mystical experience, I knew I had finally struck gold. Hundreds of mystical accounts later, I began to understand their enormous significance:

◆ The mystical experience is the most common and profound form of religious transformation known.

◆ It still happens in the world today to regular people.

◆ It is not limited or specifically connected to any particular religion, belief, or practice, nor can it be controlled in any way.

◆ It has been well described and widely documented.

- Most of all, it describes *the ultimate nature of reality* that is here with us *all the time.*

Reserved for neither prophets nor profligates, seekers nor saints, the holy nor the mad, the major mystical experience simply happens—sometimes to those who have practiced a spiritual discipline conscientiously for years, more often unexpectedly to disbelievers and the devout alike. As we saw in Jerry's account, this encounter with Presence is typically effortless, timeless, luminous, and ecstatic. Repeatedly characterized as ineffable, it is beyond the scope of language to describe, beyond the capability of mind to fully comprehend, and beyond the grasp of personal will to evoke, yet it provides a life-affirming view of a divinely infused world transcending all dualities. Unique each time and always profoundly impactful, the mystical experience leaves the individual feeling blessed, humbled, filled with wonder, and gifted with an absolutely authoritative sense of the spiritual meaning and purpose of life. Unfortunately, it is always transient, returning the awestruck soul to everyday life and all its pedestrian issues; no one retires in enlightenment.

The most important spiritual encounter a human

being can ever have, the mystical experience momentarily lifts the veil of fear, ignorance, and confusion, revealing the world to be a miraculous and overflowing effulgence of God's Presence and Being. Life, then, is no longer a problem to be solved or overcome but a continuously unfolding transparency of the world's sacred nature. Whenever it occurs, in a church, field, theater, or home, alone or in a crowd, the mystical experience is a timeless revelation of extraordinary beauty, nearly uncontainable joy, and ultimate spiritual knowledge. Described since the dawn of time and recorded history, it is the universal origin of religion, human values, and the ultimate meaning of life itself.

With the mystical experience now in bold relief, let's turn to its astounding revelations about the world and the nature of spiritual life.

Revelations of the Mystical Experience

Like the near-death experience, the full-blown mystical experience is a storehouse of extraordinary perception, realization, and wisdom, leading to some radical and liberating propositions on the spiritual nature of life. Examined carefully and seriously, it calls for a dramatic paradigm shift in our usual perception and understanding of the world, a vision I want to begin to elaborate for you now. Read and reread the following revelations slowly and thoughtfully. Each is derived directly from one or more mystical experiences. Although many defy our collective religious and reality beliefs, they are in fact sacred insights repeated by mystical writers from every era and religion. Consider this collection of revelations with an open mind. One day you may be able to confirm them for yourself in mystical consciousness.

The mystical experience reveals that existence and the entire cosmos is a single living, conscious, intelligent Presence—here, now, aware, and alert. The universe is alive and conscious! The mystical experience is direct contact with this Presence and its manifest Being.

There is no place you can go where the Presence is not. Our customary state of consciousness, clouded with constant thought and self-centered preoccupation, is the barrier to experiencing it.

The Presence encountered in the mystical experience is repeatedly described as infinitely intelligent, omniscient, loving, compassionate, timeless, and unchanging.

In the Presence, reality itself is transfigured,

revealing creation to be an amazing and radiant state of Divine Being. Eden is not another world; it is this world experienced *in the Presence.*

The mystical experience is actually an intensification of the reality that exists around us all the time. It is our obstructed consciousness that prevents us from seeing Creation.

Experienced with the purest awareness, reality is perfectly described by the ancient Hindu equation "existence=consciousness=bliss." Happiness does not depend on some future time when things will be good enough; it is the ultimate core of reality, has no other cause, and can be found most completely in the immediate, here-and-now experience of Presence and Being.

If, for one moment, you could experience the world as it truly is—radiant, precious, holy, beautiful, alive, and loving—you would know unequivocally that existence is enough.

Everyday life is itself an ongoing mystical experience potentially available to anyone.

Unaware of the Presence, we feel separate, alone, mortal, and vulnerable. To cope with the nightmare of separation, we become hardened, self-ish, and insensitive. Then the world appears to be a place of suffering and evil. As the mystics say, it is we who make the world ugly.

Searching for God contributes to the experience of separation, for it dismisses God's Presence here and now. If you believe God's Presence is other than what and where you are, your search will continue indefinitely. Similarly, if you are waiting to know God sometime in the future, you are missing God now. Eternity is *here and now,* and only in the eternal now can we experience God.

Religion, myth, and our own personal stories are attempts to understand the problem of separation, alienation, suffering, and evil. In the Presence, the need for explanations dissolves. Thomas Aquinas summarized his lifetime of theological writing as mere "straw" when he had his own late-life mystical experience.

In the Presence, one sees through experience. The problems of time, death, suffering, and evil are not what they seem, though no one can be convinced of this until they, too, come into the Presence.

The Presence is the greatest source of healing, understanding, and right action. Rather than a solution-oriented effort to solve ego-centered problems, it is a process of revelation and transformation. In fact, "problems" as we view them don't really exist in the Presence.

Who you think you are is a fiction separating you from the direct awareness of God as your very nature, substance, and consciousness. We are literally made of the Divine, for God is the *Being* of our own being. It is not that you and only you are God (which would be ridiculous grandiosity), but that God is every being.

Each of us incarnates specific attributes of the sacred. Directly felt and known, this realization evokes boundless creativity, freedom, and joy.

The full mystical experience is a taste of "cosmic consciousness," a state in which all knowledge is present and available. Because of the tremendous limitations of the human mind, very little of this ultimate knowledge is retained afterwards.

One of the great purposes of life is to know God directly. Spiritual growth is the process of experiencing the Presence firsthand and integrating more and more its consciousness and teachings into "ordinary" life.

Through mystical experience, human beings glimpse the timeless and already existing unity of heaven and earth, which is the symbolic basis of the near-universal religious belief in a second coming or return of a divine order.

Conclusions

As you can see, the mystical experience yields some extraordinary revelations about the true nature of reality, insights that will be elaborated extensively as we proceed. Whatever doubts, questions, or criticism you have so far, try to contain them for now. Remember, the whole purpose of developing mystical consciousness is to confirm these revelations for yourself. So, get ready; you are about to experience the Presence.

Chapter Two

Experiencing the Presence

God is an unknown Being beyond this world only for the indolent, the decisionless, the lethargic, the man enmeshed in his own designs; for the one who chooses, who decides, who is aflame with his goal, who is unconditioned, God is the closest, the most familiar Being that man, through his own action, realizes ever anew. . . . Whether God is "transcendent" or "immanent" does not depend on Him; it depends on man.[4]

—Martin Buber

"Where can I go from your spirit?
Or where can I flee from your presence?
If I ascend to heaven, you are there;
if I make my bed in Sheol, you are there.
If I take the wings of the morning
and settle at the farthest limits of the sea,
even there your hand shall lead me,
and your right hand shall hold me fast."[5]

—Psalm 139:7–10

ON A SPIRITUAL RETREAT in the Santa Cruz
Mountains several years ago, I walked late one afternoon in the dry and deserted California hills. I was
thinking intensely about God. Many times I called
out silently: "God, I know You are here. Where are
You? I need You." On and on I hiked, higher and higher
into the dusty sunlit hills. Coming around a corner, I
sensed it distinctly: a Presence in the wilderness, everywhere. I was stunned. But there was more. I sensed
the Presence was aware of me too, and that it was
aware that I was aware of it.

A most startling experience! I had stumbled upon
the consciousness of the universe: awesome, omnipresent, and other than my own. I had sensed the
Presence of God. This was the beginning of an ongoing exploration of mystical consciousness, a study
of the phenomenology of Presence which would intensify, differentiate, and unfold for years, eventually
growing so physically near and emotionally intimate
that it would at times merge with and be none other
than my own presence. We'll talk more about this
later.

Here I want to focus on you. The divinely conscious
world described in Chapter 1 will remain merely a
fascinating idea until you, too, can learn to sense the
Presence. So the question arises, and it is one of the

most important questions of religious life: If the divine Presence is everywhere, how do you experience it intentionally and directly? The distinction between mystical consciousness and mystical experience now becomes central because the cultivation of mystical consciousness leads directly into the experience of the Presence. Let's begin to examine what this means.

The Nature of Presence

Becoming conscious of God's Presence does not require the full-blown mystical experience described in the Introduction. In mystical consciousness, Presence is potentially discernible everywhere. But to locate it, we need specific knowledge of the experience we are looking for and a genuine desire—actually more like an urgency—to actually meet the infinite Consciousness that surrounds, lives, and holds us all.

"Okay," you say, "I can heighten and focus my awareness, but how do I recognize God's Presence? What do I actually feel or sense?" These pivotal questions challenged me for years. Very few books address them, and even those which do provide minimal if any discussion of the "how" and the "what" of this process. Given the paucity of specific directions, we first need to explore the nature of presence in general.

Begin with your own presence. What is it? Where

is it? How do you describe it? What are its qualities? Is it associated with your body? Take your time and keep exploring your subjective experience before reaching any conclusions.

Consider next the presence of another person. Pick anyone you know well. Is his or her presence determined by words, mood, energy, appearance, knowledge, wealth, attitude, or state of mind? Pick another person. How does that person's presence differ from the first person? Now consider a wider range of examples: What does it feel like to be in the presence of an infant, a salesman, a depressed person, a butcher, a priest, an alcoholic, your lover, an old woman, a murderer, a dying parent, or a crowd of 100,000 people at a football game? How are these experiences of presence different? How are they alike? What about the presence of a tree, bird, groundhog, pebble, fish, canyon, forest, or cloud?

Are you getting the idea? Everything has a presence, an experiential quality that we can learn to tune in to directly. So does God. The importance of exploring your own presence, the presence of others, and the presence of animals, things, and places is to sharpen your awareness of presence so you can know what you are looking for.

The Experiential Qualities of God's Presence

Now we can turn to the sacred Presence. How is it different from your own presence or the presence of another? Here again, the answers need to be found through careful firsthand observation. In my own experience, and my reading of the mystical literature, God's Presence has a number of rather consistent and distinct experiential qualities that grow stronger with repeated contact. Below is a fairly exhaustive list meant to facilitate your exploration. This list is not a prescription. Its purpose is simply to help you become familiar with what you might experience as you cultivate mystical consciousness.

Read these descriptions slowly, carefully—perhaps several times. Read them first for content, then for an intuitive sense of what it is you will soon experience. Take your time. As you go through them, see if you notice any "aha" reactions when you know exactly what I mean because you have already had the experience. The list is subdivided into qualities specifically associated with (1) Locating and Entering the Presence, (2) The Experience of Presence, (3) The Value of Presence, and (4) Understanding the Nature of God Through the Experience of Presence. After finishing the list, I will share one of my own experiences of Presence and then guide you into your own.

There will also be many more opportunities for experiencing the Presence in later chapters.

The Qualities and Dynamics of Presence

The Presence is a personal, subjective, here-and-now, one-of-a-kind encounter with God. It is not something that we can mechanically replicate, imitate, or model from another person's experience. You have to have the experience to know it. Though the experience will be new each time, there are familiar features that we gradually learn to recognize and trust.

Locating and Entering the Presence

The Presence is located most distinctly in the stillness, silence, and timelessness that pervade everything in the present moment. It is often associated with the realization that space itself is conscious and alive.

Locating the Presence involves the sharpening and heightening of awareness associated with mystical consciousness. The immediacy and aliveness of surrounding space is sensed with a keen, penetrating, and thoughtless awareness, as if trying to "feel" the presence of another person in a pitch-black room. The only difference is that we are sensing the aliveness of space itself.

The Presence is, indeed, the actual experience of another, except this "Other" is the very consciousness of the universe. It is sensed as an alert and awakened awareness (hence a Presence) but without any localized physical source. One needs to keep sensing into the surrounding space until this consciousness is actually felt.

The Presence we discover is beyond thought, beliefs, feelings, images, or imaginings. It is not something we conjure up nor is it found through visualization or active imagination exercises. The Presence must be encountered directly as a real and tangible consciousness pervading all reality.

We can come into the Presence in countless ways (e.g., through prayer, meditation, scriptural or inspirational reading), and it's really not the specific activity but the state of consciousness that matters. When we cease our chronic preoccupation with thought, self, time, and productivity; quiet the mind; and focus awareness into the imminent Divine here and now, the possibility of experiencing the Presence increases.

Like the experience "On Golden Pond," we also become aware of the Presence unexpectedly in the silence between thoughts, when activity and rumination cease. These shifts in the clarity of awareness happen all the time, though we rarely take advantage of them. Suddenly, God's consciousness is right here, close and available. Instead of staying present, however, we usually start thinking again.

Sometimes we sense the Presence in or through experiences that evoke awe, wonder, reverence, or holiness (e.g., nature or natural forces, beautiful scenes, inspiring or religious architecture or objects). These emotions are natural and automatic responses to the immediate experience of divine imminence. Catching our breath and our attention, we suddenly and intuitively sense, if only for a moment, that we are literally standing in the Presence of God.

The Presence is often discernible in extraordinary times (e.g., childbirth, close calls with danger, death), when the miracle and preciousness of life are undeniable, for the perception of the miraculous and precious is in fact the perception of the sacred.

Sometimes the Presence breaks into consciousness during non-cognitive activities (sports, dance, creativity) when the mind is filled with the feeling of Being, and at times when we literally embody one of the dimensions of Presence (e.g., love, lovemaking, compassion). In these instances, the Presence is usually overlooked or mistaken for the activity or emotions involved.

The Presence is found more often when we open our hearts in love, longing, and adoration, without expectation, desiring humbly and sincerely to know God's consciousness directly.

Once we learn to feel the Presence, we begin to find it everywhere. Then we have begun what the mystics throughout the ages have called the "practice of Presence."

Though the Presence seems to come and go, in reality it is our awareness of the Presence that comes and goes. It is especially elusive when we are emotionally upset, rushed, or caught up in ego-inflating projects, plans, and schemes. In fact, awareness of the Presence can be lost or forgotten for years at a time.

Just as the presence of another person cannot be controlled, mastered, or possessed, neither can the Presence of God. When one tries to control the Presence, it is quickly lost.

The Experience of Presence

As one first comes into the Presence, there is sometimes a noticeable increase in ambient light. Falling gently on things nearby, the light of Presence renders everything more beautiful, bright, crystal clear, and fascinating. The world is subtly but wonderfully transfigured in its soft and celestial illumination, which is, itself, the Presence.

It may be startling at first to realize that space is alive and aware, but with time, it becomes familiar and predictable. Like any new relationship, there is an initial period devoted to meeting, getting acquainted, and exploring the relationship until it feels familiar, comfortable, trustworthy, and intimate.

Once it is located, people often begin to describe the Presence as sweet, intimate, gentle, loving, forgiving, unconditional, uncritical, accepting, and patient. It is never tired, disinterested, frustrated, or angry. Always waiting for us, the Presence is the ultimate intimacy, empathy, and mercy.

As we let the experience of the Presence come closer, surrounding and touching us like the warm softness of a blanket, we often begin to feel peaceful, content, relaxed, and safe. There is no fear, time urgency, or worry in this loving and protected space. It feels like whatever happens will be okay, for everything is held in God's eternal love, a profoundly comforting and reassuring experience. Tremendous relief is experienced as everyday burdens are finally put down, if only for a few minutes.

As the Presence draws closer, we may feel that it touches, merges, penetrates, or even temporarily replaces our personal sense of presence. Like two gases mixing, our own individual presence and the Presence may seem to become so interpenetrated that they are one.

Experiencing this closeness or oneness with

Presence often evokes immense joy, which some describe as the soul's response to its re-union and renewed intimacy with God.

We are often moved to spontaneity by the Presence. Whether in dance, song, creativity, service, lovemaking, or even mundane activi-ties like cleaning or yard work, when the Presence surrounds, enters, or awakens us, whatever we do is transformed into a flowing, joyous, generous, unpremeditated, and even sacred process. In emergencies, too, we may be moved by Presence to perform acts tran-scending all fears about personal safety.

In the Presence, we are also more apt to *see* the Presence shining all around us, particu-larly in people, animals, and nature. Faces be-come beautiful and radiant, personalities more miraculous and wonderful, colors of growing things more vibrant. Simply put, the world be-comes more beautiful in the Presence.

The Value of Presence

Spending time in the Presence changes us, making us more like the Presence itself. In-creasingly, we take on its nature: calm, serene, patient, loving, accepting, kind, and aware of the beauty and value of everyday life, the world, and all living things.

Entering the Presence is not about getting something specific (e.g., the solution to a problem, relief from hardship, wisdom), though that can happen. Entering and being in the Presence is itself enough. It is the end of our search. There is no greater goal or purpose.

Time in the Presence, however, *is* healing. Cradled in the experienced kindness of God, we recognize the error of our self-centered ways; our violent emotions gradually melt away. Upsets are seen for what they are: misunderstandings that are temporary, self-created, and misleading. Holding every human drama is always the holiness of Presence—calm, silent, peaceful, eternal, and loving—a sanctuary we can return to anytime.

Presence does not "fix" our life dramas in the conventional sense; rather, it profoundly changes our perception of them. When problems are experienced in the serenity, kindness, understanding, and forgiveness of the Presence, we see behind others' masks of hatred and blame into their vulnerability and woundedness. Then harsh judgment is replaced by empathy, vindictiveness dissolves into caring, and eventually every part of the problem is affected (though not necessarily in the ways we preconceive).

Time, story, and the soap-opera quality of life all disappear in the Presence. In God, life is not a linear sequence of past, present, and future, a problem to be solved, or a goal to be reached; it is the eternal "now" opening like a flower into the mystical experience of Being.

The Presence is a sea of love meant to hold, guide, and sustain us through all the apparent trials of life. Spiritual maturity and mystical consciousness gradually allow us to become conduits for its love, compassion, and wisdom.

Consciousness filled with Presence is the source of all genuine and spiritually enlightened (rather than self-serving) action. From its depths flow the most authentic and loving responses we can have to the people and situations of our lives.

The Presence is also something we share with each other. This is one of its most powerful gifts, for being in the Presence together magnifies all its qualities. Then, peace, joy, compassion, and love not only melt the divisions between us, they flow through us into the world. This is the most powerful source of social action.

The Presence is not an achievement to be had, put away, and kept like a possession, souvenir, or pressed flower nor is it a belief we cling to for comfort and security. It is always new, fresh, and unfolding, opening into the Divine. As such, it is the ongoing source and essence of life.

Understanding the Nature of God Through the Experience of Presence

The Presence is timeless and unchanging. It is the same Presence experienced by Buddha, Jesus, Mohammed, and Lao-tzu. It is the same Presence you will know, and the one your great-grandchildren will know. Presence is the pervasive, unchanging, and infinite consciousness in which the entire human drama of time and history are enacted. In fact, in the consciousness of Presence, time and history do not exist.

Humankind's understanding of Presence, however, changes over the millennia because it is always colored by the psychology, culture, reality beliefs, and personal experiences of those who describe it. The contradictions found within and between religions arise from these factors and our inherently limited capacity to comprehend the fullness of God.

Because knowing God completely is beyond the capacity of the human mind, we experience the Divine in many discrete and sometimes contradictory forms including (1) a personal and imminent Presence, (2) a transcendent entity beyond this world, (3) the pure consciousness in which everything arises, (4) an impersonal force recognized through its orderliness (e.g., scientific laws), (5) a void from which everything forms and returns, and (6) an existence itself (i.e., manifest creation). Ironically, these beliefs and their contradictions become unimportant in the Presence, for it is God that we meet, not our ideas of God.

The Presence shows us what God is and, by extension, what we are. Eventually, we realize that our own presence is actually part of, one with, and the same as *the* Presence—sacred consciousness seemingly distributed individually yet always one. Awareness of one's own presence, therefore, can also be a doorway into the Presence, for as mystics from all religions perennially attest, Presence is our true and essential identity. As personal boundaries dissolve, Presence is all that remains.

Presence is itself one of the greatest arguments for the existence of God, for it is the existence of God directly experienced. A profound understanding of God's nature flows directly from this experiential encounter.

A Personal Description of Presence

To help you further anticipate what it might feel like to be in the Presence, I offer a personal account. Keep in mind, this description is not the "correct" or only way to feel the Presence; it is simply the unfolding of my own mystical consciousness. You will experience yours. Read it slowly with an open, receptive mind. Don't think, don't judge, don't analyze, just let it flow through you.

Sitting alone at the keyboard, I become still. I intentionally stop my thoughts and sharpen the focus of my perception on the sensory here-and-now. Suddenly, I *see* the world. Oh, it was there before, but I was paying no attention to it. Now reality strikes my consciousness, and the world outside my window seems to "burst in" full of beauty, color, and clarity. It's as if consciousness just "clicked" in, and I startle at all that's really around me. The house and room are peaceful; bright sunlit colors from the yard stream in through the window pane, and a breeze moves gently through the trees on this summer morning. But I want the Presence. I tune in more keenly to the deep silence around me. There is something there.

"God," I whisper under my breath, "I know You are here." Focusing more intensely, my awareness heightens, sharpening to pinpoint clarity, sensing space itself. Only the present moment exists, here, now, exactly as it is, crystal clear and lucid. It has the feel of eternity.

The room has become even more quiet and still. Time and its artificial urgencies dissolve in this expanding moment, which is, like pure consciousness, without beginning, end, thought, memory, preference, or goals. Now I sense something else: this empty, unencumbered space is itself somehow alive, awake, and alert—conscious like me. My sharpened, searching awareness has sensed the very sentience of existence. There is an actual Presence in the room now—

gentle, intelligent, aware, and everywhere, and it senses me. And knows me.

The room brightens noticeably. Light falls on my messy desk, its softness illuminating each separate thing and ever so gently touching my hands. Everything becomes visually distinct, rich in detail, color, texture, pattern, and boundary, like one of those photographs with supernatural detail—vividly beautiful. It is as if the Presence has both brightened the world and become the radiant hyperreality of everything.

I keep my awareness wide open, naked, radically here-and-now, tuning into this everywhere-centered "Other." As I do, the Presence feels so incredibly gentle, tender, kind and compassionate, and happy, like a devotedly attuned and adoring mother—understanding, holding, and accepting me with quiet yet unlimited love, as soft as this sunlight streaming through the window. I am enveloped in a sweet, private, delicious intimacy, closer than close. Taking the Presence inside my heart now becomes a love affair of exquisite, almost unbearable joy. It is all I can do to just sit with it.

Slowly, consciously, deliberately, I talk, write, share what I'm feeling, what's happening in my life, where I'm hurting or troubled. I do it slowly so that I don't leave the experience or get in my head, so that I can be conscious of every word, and the Presence holds it all. If I ask questions, the Presence often responds from a consciousness now seemingly united with my own, offering thoughts that surprise, guide, support, and love me.

I can also take the Presence into my body, where it seems to spread like a wave, individual rivulets flowing especially into places where I feel most weary or wounded. As the energy of Presence fills me, I become wondrously relaxed and peaceful, held in this gentle, infinitely loving kindness, and a feeling of healing moves through me, slowly restoring my depleted being. Over and over again I express my gratefulness, for I know absolutely that I have done nothing to deserve this healing, yet it is always here, waiting, and giving so generously. I am so humbled.

Gradually, I begin to feel as if my own presence and being were not only permeated by the Presence, but somehow composed of it. Gratefully, I allow the exhausting pretense of "personhood" to melt into the holiness of Being, replacing the struggle of separateness with the profoundly relaxing and luxurious experience of oneness. My body now is alive as God; my being has become God's Being. This unity evokes bursts of ecstasy, more than I can bear, as if I had touched the very source of life and exploded into uncontainable joy. I thank God profusely, express my overflowing love, and know there is nothing more I could ever want.

Now the experience of Presence is everywhere and perfect. I see that all this is God: every thing, person, sound, event, sensation, feeling, breath, movement, and moment. Nothing is left out and nothing needs fixing. This moment is enough. The world is alive, joyous, and precious. I sense, too, that whatever happens—even sickness, loss, death, and disaster—happens in this perfect, loving, and eternal Presence. In fact, in this living, conscious, joyous Reality, it doesn't really matter what happens. Held, nourished, and caressed in this infinite love, I surrender my entire life, all its parts and outcomes, and merge into an immense experience of contentment and peace.

Eventually, when I've had all I need (or can bear), I thank God and feel ready to move quietly back into the life going on around me: family, work, chores, whatever it is. Carrying the peace and serenity with me, I approach people and "problems" with more patience, kindness, and forgiveness. This loving and generous feeling may not always stay long (it's amazing how quickly certain "problems" can trigger my reactivity), but I know that I have been in God, and I know I am better for it.

The depth and reality of this experience surprise me anew each time. I am repeatedly awed and wonder how and why I drift so far away from the Presence every day. And I realize more and more that nothing important is worth doing without first being bathed, infused, and transformed in this infinite sanctity of Presence. I pray intently to live ever more consciously and constantly in its loving awareness. But whatever happens, however I advance or fail, I know that this experience is enough. In this union, free of thought, mind, and individuality, I behold all reality as holy, permeated with God's love and consciousness and move gratefully into the divine stream of Being.

Experiencing the Presence: Your Turn

Several years ago I began a spiritual friendship with a wonderful, open-hearted priest. Spiritual friendship is an intentional alliance based on sharing and facilitating each other's relationship with God. In a safe and prayerful atmosphere, we talk about our subjective experience of the Divine—in our lives and in the moment. Like my breakfast with Eric, this kind of spiritual sharing often brings us directly into the sacred. One day, early in our visits, my friend said gently, "Now let us enter the Presence." His words startled me. In a way, it was that simple: Shift your attention and come into the Presence. And there it was again, in the room, all around us. Now it's your turn to enter the Presence.

Below is an exercise devoted to experiencing the Presence. Keep in mind that mystics talk about "practicing the Presence" because it involves an incremental process of learning to shift into (and stay in) the awareness we have called mystical consciousness. By this time, I hope you are beginning to have an intuitive feel for what the experience of Presence might be like. Don't worry about being right or perfect. Give yourself full permission to have your own, unique experience. Simply follow these instructions patiently, openly, reverently, and see what takes place. Stay with each step until you have experienced something of the described state. You are about to enter into the holiness of Presence. Do so with a sincerely religious attitude.

There are six parts to the exercise: Entering the Present, Sensing the Presence, Entering Presence, Letting the Presence Enter You, Finding the Presence Within, and Developing a Daily Relationship With the Presence. Designed to be done sequentially, these steps will gradually bring you into as continuous a relationship with the Presence as you desire or can bear. Take all the time you need, repeat the steps as often as necessary to really get inside the experience, and don't try to complete the entire sequence in one sitting. Keep in mind that the moment you become impatient or impose your own plans, expectations, or deadlines on the timeless space of divine experience, you leave the Presence.

Step One: Entering the Present

Sit in a quiet, solitary place undistracted by music, television, noises, or worries. Be sure you have enough time to forget entirely about time.

Cease all activity and become still. No thinking, no analyzing, and no manipulating this experience.

Become very alert, awake, and focused, opening into a state of pure sensory awareness, entirely free of thoughts, expectations, beliefs, memories, and self-concerns.

Heighten and sharpen your awareness even more, perceiving everything with crystal clarity. Look at the world as if for the very first time—new, fresh, unfamiliar, and amazing.

Notice how the world brightens, becoming more beautiful, colorful, three dimensional, and fascinating. Notice that each thing you really look at is wondrously and indescribably perfect in itself.

Now become aware of the space that surrounds and penetrates everything. Tune in to it. See if you can feel its existence and essence.

Stay present in this heightened, clarified, thoughtless awareness. Be conscious of consciousness itself. You are very close to sensing the Presence.

Step Two: Sensing the Presence

Probe the surrounding space with your heightened consciousness. See if you can actually begin to sense an awareness, not your own, all around you. This is like sensing the presence of another person in a pitch-black room: you know the person is there. The Presence is there too.

You might whisper quietly, or silently, something like, "God, I know You are here" or simply repeat whatever word you use for the Divine several times, sensing what happens in the room as you say it. Don't get lost in your words; it's the consciousness around you that's important.

Notice how you begin to sense space or reality becoming alive with the sentience of Presence. Perhaps you have a sense of being seen or heard by an intelligence that fills the room. Keep trying until you begin to experience some aspect of the "Other."

Notice, too, that this awareness you are tuning in to already knows you and is aware that you are aware of it. Focus on this direct experience of mutual knowing. It is the first step in developing a conscious relationship with the Presence.

Now see if you can feel the Presence in the space closest to you. It's sometimes most easily sensed within a few feet or inches of your body. As you experience the Presence that close, it may begin to feel warm, gentle, kind, intimate, and loving.

If you are having trouble with this step, try going someplace where Presence is more easily experienced. For example, the Presence is often more discernible in natural places: the woods, a sunlit meadow, the park, or the garden behind your house (see also an exercise called "Communing With the Divine in Nature" in Chapter 6). Or, you might sense the Presence more easily while sitting quietly in a church or visiting a holy place.

Step Three: Entering the Presence

Sense yourself surrounded, touched, and known by this gentle, loving, invisible consciousness. You may actually feel its love warming the room, caressing your skin, flowing over your being.

Come further into this Presence the way you would come into the presence of another person. Experience its energy and be sensitively attuned to the attitude, mood, and feeling tone it creates around you. Trust what you sense.

Allow yourself now to be drawn into loving communion. Talk slowly, quietly, and intimately to the Presence, sharing your life, feelings, and prayers. Let your heart and soul be touched by this One that holds you so tenderly.

Begin to explore your relationship with the Presence. For example, see what happens in this moment-by-moment process when you express love, praise, or gratitude. Do your feelings affect the Presence? Does being in the Presence change or affect you?

Continue in this very subjective, experiential process. Be very careful not to lose the Presence by thinking about what is happening, and don't lapse into fantasy. Remember, this experience is beyond ideas, beliefs, and imaginings. You may at first sense the Presence, lose it, then sense it again. There is an art to being in the consciousness of God, but you must learn to perfect it for yourself.

Step Four: Letting the Presence Enter You

Now take the Presence inside you. Feel your physical being saturated with the feeling, energy, and being of this Being. Notice how you can actually feel it moving within and through you.

Notice, too, how an experience of union begins to happen in this merging: your presence increasingly becoming one with the Presence, your being becoming one with divine Being. As you feel this oneness, gratefully relinquish your separate, worried, problem-ridden self into the divine Other.

Feel the joy, relief, and freedom that accompany giving up the burden of self and identity, allowing the Presence to be who you are. It is not that you alone are God or that God has commandeered your personality or that you now have all God's power—these are all foolish stories we've been told, which keep us from this union—only that pure consciousness and being are the experience of God.

Here is one more optional step. Stand up. Begin walking slowly, consciously, very deliberately, fully present, feeling God flowing through your movements, thoughts, and perceptions. Live this moment as the Presence living you.

Step Five: Finding the Presence Within

The Presence can also be approached from the inside. In fact, the "God within" has been the more common and traditional way people experience the Presence, often through meditative and contemplative practices. You may discover this inner path to be easier or harder. Remember, there is no right or wrong way to meet God. Whatever you experience is simply the way it is for you at this time. Again, take all the time you need; you can't hurry this experience. You may also wish to tape-record these instructions, spacing the individual directives at one- or two-minute intervals, to avoid having to open your eyes to read them.

Close your eyes and quiet your mind. If you have trouble silencing your thoughts, practice some form of meditation like watching your thoughts without reacting to them until you can focus on the inner stillness.

Heighten awareness and concentration, probing and exploring your interior space with a clear focus. Avoid fantasy and imagination.

Consider that this inner space is not only permeated with Presence, *it is the Presence.* You are that close to the consciousness of the universe. You might silently whisper, "I know You are here," "I know this is You," or repeat your name for the Divine a few times. Stay keenly present and don't start thinking.

Have no expectations about what you should experience. Whatever you are experiencing beyond thought and imagination is the Presence or that part of the Presence you are capable of knowing right now. Try to experience it *as it is*, not what you think it should be.

Feel and explore this inner Presence. What are some of its qualities? Is it silent, spacious, time-less, calm, powerful, gentle, warm, dark, light? Does it move? What is its awareness like? How do you react to its existence?

Deepen this union. Let the Presence mingle and merge with your presence and body until there is only one. Collapse, surrender, or simply rest in it for as long as you need. This sacred and tender darkness is always there to heal, soothe, and restore you when you take the time to experience it.

Realize, again, that the divine Being is the being of your own body, and then forget yourself entirely. When you cease being you, cease doing your identity and personality, what is left is the Divine. You are not only filled with God, you are God's very substance and life. Feeling your own experience of being, remind yourself: "This is God."

Let this inner Presence be your most intimate companion. Feel it caressing, loving, pervading, and lightening your being. Cherish and respond to it in return like a secret inner lover. This can be such a sweet, intimate, and joyous experience. But keep this relationship to yourself, for this communion grows in secrecy, darkness, silence, and solitude.

Quietly and inwardly, talk to the Presence. Share your innermost needs and feelings. Release all that you struggle with into it.

Feel the Presence in places of physical or emotional pain, fatigue, or deadness. Notice how it gradually permeates, softens, and brings healing to the places that hurt.

As you are made of Presence and Being, realize now that everything is. Before you open your eyes, "see" the world and all life simply as variations of what you are, allowing you to understand the spiritual commandment to love your neighbor as yourself. Have compassion also for those who identify solely with their fictional selves and must endure the suffering created by all their erroneous beliefs.

When you have had enough time in the Presence, come back out, open your eyes, see the world anew. Let this transformed inner being be you.

Finally, notice how your perception, beliefs, and behavior change in this joyous union. How do you become more loving, compassionate, and forgiving, especially in situations currently difficult for you?

Step Six: Developing a Daily Relationship With the Presence

If you are willing to go further, develop an ongoing relationship with the Presence by spending time in it every day. Your experience will evolve and deepen with practice.

Be sure to take care of this relationship. Like any valued friendship, its authenticity and depth depend on the continuing respect, sincerity, and genuine attention you bring to it.

Enter the Presence whenever you are hurt, confused, or off balance—when you need to prepare for something difficult or make a tough decision. See how it changes your entire orientation to whatever problem is facing you. But be sure to take your time, have no expectations, and make no demands. Let the Presence change you.

As you "practice the Presence" over time, notice especially what contributes to finding, losing, and refinding it again in your daily life.

Notice, too, how you are changing. What do you discover about your own nature in the process? What is the Presence teaching you?

Review

What have you learned so far from this experiential process of sensing and entering the Presence? What surprised you? Did something happen that you distrusted, disbelieved, and discounted? What was it? In your journal, describe what you experienced. Collect observations every time you use these instructions so that you can watch your experience evolve. Try not to discount, minimize, or judge what takes place. You are experiencing God; let it happen in its own way.

What the Presence Is Not

Remember, the Presence is real. This is not visualization, imagination, problem-solving, self-improvement, or an attempt to get God to change something; nor is it simply a "feel good," need-gratification, or relaxation exercise, or an escape from pain and ordinary life responsibilities. Practicing the Presence is its own end: a melting into the peace and serenity of eternity beyond the world's concern for survival, efficiency, productivity, and success. Though the Presence may transform your life, sometimes even produce extraordinary changes, results are not the reason we come to God. It is God alone that we seek. However your life changes, or doesn't change, matters little. Rest in the Presence and then return to the world as it is, with gratitude, seeing that it, too, is God. Everything follows naturally from here. This is the contemplative life.

Chapter Three

Presence as the World: Being and the Return to Eden

Closely connected with the sense of the "Presence of God" . . . is the complementary mark of the illuminated consciousness; the vision of "a new heaven and a new earth," or an added significance and reality in the phenomenal world. . . . It takes, as a rule, the form of an enhanced mental lucidity—an abnormal sharpening of the senses—whereby an ineffable radiance, a beauty and a reality never before suspected, are perceived by a sort of clairvoyance shining in the meanest things.[6]

—Evelyn Underhill

This is it, this is Eden. When you see the kingdom spread upon the earth, the old way of living in the world is annihilated. That is the end of the world. The end of the world is not an event to come, it is an event of psychological transformation, of visionary transformation. You see not the world of solid things but a world of radiance.[7]

—Joseph Campbell

If on earth there be
    a Paradise of Bliss,
It is this,
It is this,
It is this.[8]

                   —Firdausi

THERE ARE DAYS when I step out of my home or office and find myself nearly jolted by the sheer intensity of the world, as if energy were pouring through the sky, clouds, trees, light, and air, and blasting me with its awesome force. Have you ever had that experience? This is the force of Being: Presence perfusing Creation, transforming the world into a place of unbelievable beauty, magic, and power. Being, God's physical manifestation in and as the world, is therefore another way we can know the Divine. What does this mean, and how can we experience God's Being directly?

Science and everyday experience tell us that the universe is a dynamic physical process. From subatomic particles to the endless spiraling of galaxies, everything is "alive" with energy, motion, and change. The dynamic quality of the physical world is well captured by the word *being*, the present participle "ing" emphasizing its constant activity. Scientists also tell us that the physical world itself one day produced life, evolving from microorganisms to plants, animals, and human "beings." Now parts of being itself were literally alive and conscious! Then, as if this were not miracle enough, the mystical experience tells us that the whole universe is alive and divine (and always has been) and that the Presence not only shines through the world, it is the world. The word *Being* expresses the living, sacred nature of everything, capitalized to connote its divinity. Reality is sacred substance, made of and permeated by God. In mystical consciousness, even rocks are made of God.

Now the mystical understanding of Being takes one more incredible step. In the Presence, not only does being become Being, but everyday reality is transfigured. With perception wiped clean of time, self, and mind, we literally find ourselves back in the biblical paradise of Eden. The mystics say that if we could, but for a nanosecond, experience the infinite holiness of the world we are in right now, we would fall instantly to our knees, kiss the ground, and proclaim, *"It is this, It is this, It is this."* Then the world shines again as the original Garden, restoring Creation and opening the gates of heaven.

The Garden is a universal idea found throughout the creation stories of the world's myths and religions. It refers to a time when the Earth itself was a divine paradise. In fact, the word *paradise* comes from the ancient Iranian *pairidaeza*, meaning a walled or enclosed garden. In the sacred Garden, Heaven and Earth were not separate, Spirit was alive in everything, a close and natural communion existed between humanity and God (or the spirit world), and humans still displayed a saintliness of character. As most creation myths portray, however, people invariably succumbed to pride, greed, and disobedience, rejecting, losing, and then forgetting the Garden after which all manner of catastrophes and suffering occurred. Usually there is a related prophecy of a future paradise, a return to paradise, or a heavenly paradise found after death. Entrance into the Garden, however, always requires a major purification process.

Ordinary Enlightenment argues that the Garden is more than a myth, that it actually represents a perception of the ultimate nature of the world. The Garden is found when the world is experienced with senses heightened and wiped clean of mind, time, and self. With naked and intense awareness, we will discover a magical, unspeakably beautiful, luminous, and holy place *all around us*! This ultimate reality is called the "Pure Land" by Buddhists, the "Kingdom of God" by Christians, and the "Garden of Shiva" by Hindus. Remember, it was poet William Blake who said, "If the doors of perception were cleansed every thing would appear to man as it is, infinite." When you really see this miraculous world in heightened consciousness with fresh and loving eyes, you find that it is still Creation. It has always been here. In fact, we saw it once in childhood. As William Wordsworth recalled in his ode "Intimations of Immortality from Recollections of Early Childhood":

> There was a time when meadow, grove, and
> stream,
> The earth, and every common sight,
> To me did seem
> Apparelled in celestial light,
> The glory and the freshness of a dream.
>
> "Heaven," he argued, "lies about us in our
> infancy."

Unfortunately, this perception of ultimate reality is always lost. Wordsworth lamented,

> It is not now as it hath been of yore;—
> Turn wheresoe'er I may,
> By night or day,
> The things which I have seen I now can see
> no more.[9]

We have all "lost" Eden. As the myth goes, we, too, succumbed to pride, greed, and disobedience, trading the perceptual innocence of paradise for a man-made world of glamour and excitement. We have forgotten how to see. Indeed, reality "perceived" through our unenlightened eyes can be a pretty scary place, rampant with disease, poverty, danger, and hatred. In the ruthlessness of the workplace, the poverty of the inner city, or the obscene materialism of western life, it can sometimes be difficult to believe that God exists at all. The stark contrast between the world of the mystical experience and the one we see through everyday eyes will be discussed later (Chapter 7). For now, hold your questions and reservations, for the *experience* of Being as Eden must precede any debate about it, or we'll be lost outside its gates forever.

How do we experience Being and Eden directly? What psychological or visionary transformation will allow us to confirm that the Kingdom is an already present reality? Paradise, the divinely infused world revealed in the mystical experience, can also be found and confirmed in mystical consciousness. My goal in this chapter is to bring you into the Garden-consciousness of Creation. Proof of ultimate reality will never come by logic or clever discourse, but only through direct perception. So get ready; you are about to come home.

Homecoming: The Mystical Consciousness of Being and Eden

Every day, every moment, Presence permeates reality. It is in me, in you, in the children, in the animals, woods, trees, rocks, air, and insects. Pulsating with divinity, amazing beyond anything we could preconceive, this world is the living and transparent Being of God. Gaze out your window at whatever scene is calling you: gracefully dancing trees, wild-riding wind, gently falling rain, glistening snow, hot suburban asphalt, or jet black night pierced by more stars than anyone has ever counted. Witness the beauty, color, light, and power of Being. Then, come into the Presence and really *see* this miraculous world with consciousness cleansed of mind, time, and self. If you do so, everything will be transformed: Being becomes Eden, creation opens to Creation, and existence is found to be a timeless flow of divine revelation.

This exercise is about coming home. Its purpose is to clean the lens of perception and, through the intensification of mystical consciousness, give you a glimpse of the world's ultimate nature.

A few reminders: This is not a guided imagery exercise, nor is it a test or race. You don't need to fantasize or imagine anything. Go slowly and take all the time you need. And especially don't worry about whether you are doing it right. Remember it is the thinking mind, with its filters and judgments, that suppresses mystical consciousness in the first place. You may at times want to figure this out, defeat or analyze the exercise, or even disparage it. Whatever your skeptical mind tempts you to do, don't! Instead be present, intensely aware, free of thought, and completely here. Focus on what you do experience (not on what you don't) and observe the ways your perception actually begins to change. You may simply wish to practice with one directive at a time, until the mystical consciousness and perception it describes become natural and familiar to you. Finally, don't skip any parts that seem to repeat earlier exercises. Redundancy is there to keep you practicing (and experiencing!) the Presence. Let's begin.

> Sit comfortably. Loosen any tight-fitting clothes and be sure you are free of distractions and interruptions.

> Be still for a moment, this moment, and begin to relax. Quiet your thoughts and bring your attention to a clear and sharply focused awareness. Let your thinking mind cease its activity. No future, no past, no memories, no imaginings, or no troubles. Right now, this awakened

moment is all that matters and all that exists. It is the goal of this exercise and of life.

Breathe quietly, naturally, slowly. Feel each breath as a totally new and complete experience. Don't get sleepy, dreamy, or distracted. Stay absolutely present in the here and now.

Come even more fully into the present, into pure, sensory awareness. Just sit and be radically aware of sitting as an immediate and remarkable physical experience: here, now, just as you are, nothing to change. Notice the pressure of the chair, the feel of posture and muscles, and the rhythm of breathing. Be in your body as consciously as you can.

Now amplify all sensation—listen acutely, see distinctly, touch sensitively, smell sharply—so that perception becomes rich, colorful, vivid, and vibrant.

Try this: Really look at your hands, closely. Move them slowly and intentionally in front of you. Study your skin, its wrinkles, color, pattern, and feel the movement of your arms and wrists as you turn your hands over. Now investigate something else close to you. Inspect it, see it just exactly as it is, not as an example of a class of objects you think you know all about, but simply and totally as it is right now in front of you, as a pure, fresh, new, and totally unique perceptual event.

Notice as you examine the world carefully, thoughtlessly, and thoroughly that it becomes brighter, more colorful, and striking in detail. Studied intensely as if for the very first time, each thing becomes exquisitely beautiful. Look even closer! Rembrandt could not have painted it more perfectly. But more than a painting, it is three-dimensional and incredible from every angle.

Now I want you to see your entire environment in this radical way. Look at the world around you—trees, shrubs, grass, buildings, streets—with eyes wide open to its incredible visual diversity. Notice the color of the sky and the subtle movement of clouds, leaves, animals, and sunlight. Study the outline and contrast of light and shadow everywhere. Watch people and cars as if for the very first time and be amazed at what you really see. Listen intently to the sounds in your world right now, each one new, fresh, unfiltered.

Examined in this intensified consciousness, reality—here, now, right where you are—becomes a wondrous, almost fairy-tale scene of mythic dimensions: dancing trees, living sidewalks, charming old fences, climbing vines, magical gardens, and delightful people of all shapes and types. Can you see the incredible detail and splendor of this radiant, whimsical, and divinely handcrafted reality? Complete, beautiful, hyper-real, and incredibly fascinating *just as it is.* No piece is out of place. No piece needs to be changed or improved. Everything so amazing in color, texture, and arrangement, the scene could be from the special effects of a movie, yet it is reality! The sheer beauty of this place could make you nearly ecstatic.

Walk through the world you are now seeing. Notice how scenes change as you move through them. Virtual reality—yet so real you could spend a lifetime exploring its incredible nooks and crannies.

Realize next that you, too, are part of this incredible scene. Look at yourself again. You are just as amazing. Touch your body. Marvel at its living energy, vibrancy, and capacity for sensation. Vision, hearing, touch, feel, smell, and taste are all miraculous, and even more miraculous is your capacity for consciousness, love, and enlightenment. You are perfect, just as you are, and you belong here: an irreplaceable part of the wholeness and perfection of Being and absolutely necessary to it. We are all part of this wholeness, and the beauty of this moment is beyond comprehension.

Amidst this incredible beauty and perfect "all rightness," release your chronic pattern of worry and insecurity, and instead, just for this moment, permit yourself to feel happy. Understand, there is really nothing you must do or earn to be happy. If you won the lottery, you'd know just how to feel ecstatic, immediately, without any practice. You already know how to be happy. In this garden of beauty, in this banquet of divine and abundant reality, in the ground of your own divine Being, you have won: you already have all you will ever need or want, much more than you can imagine. So, at least for this moment, be happy, joyous, enraptured, peaceful, or at least content.

The mystics tell us that reality is filled with a Presence: alive, conscious, eternal, loving, joyous, and everywhere present—permeating, brightening, and animating all things. You are in that Presence right now. All life is held in its blessing, and you are personally known and loved by it. Come further into the Presence now and sense that *Reality is this living, breathing, sacred Being:* one wondrous, seamless, indescribable whole. Can you begin, just begin, to know the world in this way?

Look even more closely at Reality: you are seeing God! God has not left creation; God *is* Creation. The place you are in is literally the divine shining and manifesting everywhere.

When the world becomes this real, this beautiful, this perfect, this luminous, you are beginning to see Eden. It is here, all around you. Reality, imminent and alive, becomes the scriptural Garden. Earth, the jewel of the solar system, the galaxy, possibly the whole cosmos, is Paradise! There is nothing else like it anywhere we know—nothing so rich, verdant, beautiful, and full of life. You never left the Garden; you just forgot how to see it, for Eden returns with a change in consciousness. Eternity is always here and now, wherever you are, and includes all time and all places. This is "Heaven on Earth" and the "Kingdom of God" that people think await somewhere else. Don't let your skeptical mind interfere because of the extraordinary nature of these ideas. You are in the Garden now.

In this acute and lucid awareness, the world becomes hyperrealistic and literally conscious. Feel the power and Presence of God flowing through reality: full, vibrating, luminous, holy.

In this sacred and precious Reality, notice that there is no good or bad, no sin or evil, and no ugliness or deprivation. In the profoundly transformed perception of mystical consciousness, wherever you are and whatever you have is more than enough: it is incredible. There is only the fullness and holiness of God.

Next, experience your own being. What does it feel like? Go beyond your physical complaints, medical conditions, or emotional states. Sense instead the underlying power of Being: the vital, alive, dynamic force of existence that is you. What does this energy or power feel like?

Now, realize this: You, too, are made of the same sacred Being. This body of yours—

these hands, their movement, your thought and breath—is all God. You are a living and potentially conscious embodiment and incarnation of the Divine. God is the very energy, presence, and consciousness of *your* being. You are not outside the Garden; you are part of the Garden. Forget your idea of self, and explore this opening to mystical union. You are this close to God.

Merging with divine Being, sense how God looks through your eyes, hears through your ears, feels through your body. What you customarily assume to be "your" consciousness is actually the Presence, breathing your breath, animating your movements, and living your body. Your body is the living God, and feeling it in this way evokes ecstasy!

The world is the Presence, Garden, and Being of God. Entering Eden requires that you cease thinking, intensify awareness, and really see what is right before your eyes. *It is this, it is this, it is this.*

Continue sitting silently for a little while longer so you can really absorb this experience.

Review

What did you see, experience, and learn from this exercise in mystical consciousness? Did your experience change the way you look at the world? The perceptual changes described may come slowly at first. No matter how subtle they may seem, keep opening yourself to this new way of seeing. Remember, too, that we all move at our own pace. If you feel dissatisfied or critical with your progress, you will only be adding another layer of negativity to your psyche and another barrier to the Divine. Instead, be thankful for whatever beauty and wisdom you experience each time. Finally, you can repeat this exercise whenever you wish. A tape recording of the text may be useful to avoid the distraction of reading.

Further Implications

Homecoming has been an increasingly fascinating exercise for me. Each time I use these skills, I seem to go more deeply into Reality, and each time I see more. For example . . .

On an errand to the store, I was struck by the bizarre overlap of our two worlds—human and divine. Superimposed on the infinite beauty of Being is the human world: buildings, signs, goals, and routinized social behavior. Insulated by cars, costumes, and customs, most of us "see" only the man-made world with its constant survival anxiety. But the sacred is nonetheless still here and palpable—shining brightly, awesomely beautiful, and generous beyond description. How tragic our forgetting!

When I am alone, especially in nature, the world becomes even more enchanting. In the heightened perceptual clarity of mystical consciousness, things take on the surreal quality of a dreamscape or mythic reality, with all the whimsy and magic of a fairy tale. Trees have personalities, the river sings, and I almost expect to see gnomes, minstrels, and castles appear around the corner. Stepping into this Celtic fairyland, I leave the culturally created world of time, identity, and responsibility and become lost in a mystical wonderland. Keep in mind, this is *not* my imagination, for I am examining everything with as much consciousness and clarity of perception as I can muster. The world is far more remarkable than we realize. The civilized human being has forgotten his or her original state of consciousness.

There is another experience that can arise when reality is examined in mystical consciousness. Sometimes everything is perceived as a construction of mind, or more profoundly, a projection of Divine Mind. In this "Reality," constituted of pure energy and light, the world appears as intensely luminous, multicolored energy. Forms are still evident (e.g., trees, shrubs, fences), but they are transparent with light. A living radiance shines through everything, as if each "thing"—even body, self, and mind—is experienced as divine, allowing one to experience the world as if from God's consciousness. These dimensions of reality are also encountered by advanced meditators, who learn to enter the purer realms of awareness and sometimes by people on mind-altering drugs.

As mystics and psychedelic travelers have hinted for centuries, any tour through the realms of consciousness eventually reveals that "reality" is actually composed of numerous realities, including the cultural-consensual reality that human beings create and reinforce for each other, the nonordinary reality experienced in dreams or altered states (e.g., psychoses, shamanic journeys, out-of-body experiences), the mystical experience (in which reality is literally transfigured into Presence, Being, and Eden), and merger with the ultimate reality beyond mind that is pure God.

So what is real, and which reality is God? From the mystical point of view, it's all God. What an incredible experience we have been given! Learn about it. Enjoy it. As a mother might tell her children on a "boring" summer day: "Go out into the world. No one should ever be bored!"

If This Were Eden . . .

The Garden is not just a nice metaphor or analogy; it is a change in consciousness, and a promise. The more constant and real the experience of Presence is for you, the more Eden will shine into your life, eventually transforming the world into an ongoing mystical experience. What would it be like to live in Eden? Here are some observations from Edenic consciousness. See if you can gradually corroborate them as your mystical consciousness develops, for the degree to which these observations are real to you is the degree you have come into Eden.

> The world is intensely beautiful, intrinsically fascinating, always new. Reality has so many dimensions that you could devote a whole day, a lifetime, and never see it all.

> People appear radiant, even angelic. Faces shine with an inner light. Invidious comparisons dissolve in the beauty of each person.

> With consciousness so radically open to the immediate divine present, there is nothing to

think about and no future time or place to imagine. Thought is related only to what we are actually saying or doing here and now.

Time does not exist. There is only the eternity of now.

Life is lived on holy ground for everything, and everywhere is holy. Whatever we do (e.g., music, work, conversation) is given added beauty and meaning in the Presence of God.

In Edenic consciousness, filled with Presence, we feel boundless love for everyone and everything. Living with people who cannot see Eden, however, we may limit its expression to avoid embarrassing others.

In Eden, there is no reason to control or hoard anything. Because selfishness separates us from the Presence, it is painful and unrewarding. Instead, we know that the only natural way to live is with joy, abundance, and generosity.

There is no ugliness, badness, guilt, sin, or evil here. Tremendous compassion is felt for all who cannot see its beauty and who act desperately, cruelly, and selfishly as a result. Their world is understood to be an unending (yet entirely reversible) nightmare of fear and insecurity.

Since there is nothing to resist, nothing to hang on to, and nothing to lose, suffering does not exist in mystic consciousness. If this is God, what can be won or lost? Even physical pain is experienced as a kind of ecstasy, for all sensation is an experience of the Divine.

Since there is no self to defend, no possibility of abandonment, and the ambiance of love as tangible as light, major emotional problems do not exist. Instead we learn how to experience the symphony of loving emotions that make us Divine and the harmony of all things that makes us one.

There are no established prescriptions for behavior and nothing we have to be. In fact, identity, so full of artificial expectations, is a burden gladly shed.

With no identity or fictional self-concept to separate us from the Presence or one another, we are free to experience and express our own divine nature in whatever way it blossoms.

Knowing ourselves to be Divine, there are no

secrets, nothing to hide, and no split between an inner person and outer persona. One's own being is as interesting and rewarding as the rest of the divine world, not because it proffers any personal gain or competitive edge, but simply because it is more of the Divine.

There is no dogma and no conflict over Truth or scripture. In the Presence, the steady experience of wonder and love is the only reality, leaving nothing conceptual to fight over.

Presence and Being come together so that everything, even the seemingly inanimate world, has a consciousness that can be experienced through our awakened senses. Reality is experienced as the mind, substance, and consciousness of God.

In the Presence, perception is highly intuitive, even psychic. Words are often unnecessary, for consciousness includes (and penetrates) everything, and all share in it.

Work performed in the Presence becomes a timeless, effortless flow of loving creativity, constantly contributing to the expression and enjoyment of Creation. With no attachment to self or identity, there is no concern for failure.

We don't work because we have to; we work because it feels so wonderful and right.

Learning is tremendously valued, not because it makes us smarter or more successful, but because it allows us to better understand God and revelation.

Death does not exist. Dying is understood as a transition from one experience or version of God to another. There is nothing to be afraid of: in eternity, no one dies; forms simply change, and we continue as a unique consciousness until dissolving back into the One, like individual bubbles in a bubble bath. Enjoy each form you experience, until you are ready to let go. This is the journey.

In Eden, life is a joyous and spontaneously loving dance with the Divine Being in the eternal now. The dance ends only when we forget the Presence and click back into the fictional, time-bound world of suffering and struggle projected from our confused and clouded minds.

Conclusions

Mystical consciousness finds a world transformed by Presence, a revelation of Being and Eden that can be confirmed only from within the experience. If these ideas are offensive or unbelievable, you are still in the world of conventional beliefs and everyday consciousness. Rather than discounting the Edenic world of Presence, put your energy into learning to experience mystical consciousness and then reconsider your beliefs.

Can we stay in Edenic consciousness? What about all the practicalities of making a living, taking care of responsibilities, and attending to physical survival? We'll return to these questions in the final chapter, where they will take on entirely new meaning. As you grow in mystical consciousness, you'll answer many of them for yourself.

What's next? Returning to Being and Eden is indeed an incredible homecoming. And as hinted in the exercise, there is one more step: union with the Presence. What is this ultimate experience, and is it really available to ordinary people? Chapter 4 takes us into the very heart and soul of the spiritual journey: Mystical Union.

Chapter Four

Mystical Union

Let your thoughts flow past you, calmly;
keep me near, at every moment;
trust me with your life, because I
am you, more than you yourself are.[10]
—Bhagavad Gita

True prayer is a realization that God
constitutes our being and our life.[11]
—Joel Goldsmith

MYSTICAL UNION IS FOUND in the discovery that God's Presence and Being is our own presence and being. Mystics from across traditions and eras have said this in countless ways: that God gives birth to Himself in me, that the truest Self is God, and that God is the Being of my being. One of the goals of spiritual life, therefore, is to come into this radical and immediate experience of unity. How do we understand, integrate, and experience union and incarnation into our actual lives?

Rather than try to answer this question conceptually, let me take you into my own experience. The writings from this section are derived from a fascinating experiment: they are the personal insights and revelations gleaned from dialogues with God. Holding my awareness in the mystical consciousness of Presence described in Chapter 2, I write down the thoughts, feelings, questions, and responses that arise in our intersubjective merging. Telling God what I experience is a way of clarifying my understanding of mystical communion. Recording what comes back from the Presence is a way of receiving revelation. These descriptions are not presented as the only or correct way of experiencing union; they simply reflect the subjective dynamics of union as I know it. You will discover your own version.

I have selected those particular interchanges that carry special significance and content relative to the theme of this chapter. Rereading the dialogues, I was surprised to discover that my conversations fall into several recurring categories which describe the fluid and evolving experience of separation, union, and transformation. These dialogues not only support the Bhagavad Gita quotation but also further amplify the underlying dynamics of mystical union described in Chapter 2. In respect for its source, and as an example of the practice of writing in the mystical consciousness of Presence, I include this material essentially unchanged (though pruned of unnecessary repetition).

Read these dialogues slowly and carefully. "M" refers to me and "G" to God. This section may be difficult reading because it records a flow of ideas that took place in mystical consciousness, which is altogether different than ordinary consciousness. The repetition you will notice is part of the dialogue's stumbling, unplanned, and interactive nature, reflecting my own struggle to understand the experience of merging and transformation. Try not to get distracted by the vacillating states of separation and union, duality and unity. This dialectic simply reflects the unstable and paradoxical nature of the process—first two, then one, then two, then one again—in the dance of intimacy, confluence, and absorption. Finally, no matter how strange these dialogues may seem, stay out of your skeptical, judgmental mind, for if you distance in that way, you will miss the experiential heart and soul of Ordinary Enlightenment.

The Problem of Separation

M: So much of the time what I do is false: me directing me to act like my idea of me would act . . . controlling, conforming, complying, all to fit into what I view as the human rules of acting like a person. This is a straitjacket. It cuts me off from You. I live in the world of artificial human rules, not in the consciousness of God.

G: Relax. Stop being anyone. I am your being. Stop picturing yourself as a separate mortal being. Start living as Me.

M: How can I be You?

G: By forgetting who *you* are. You want your self more than you want Me. Come to Me.

M: How?

G: By sensing Me, feeling Me, knowing Me. I am your Spirit. I am your body. I am this world. You cannot ever be far from Me, for I am all you are. It is only your self-interest and preoccupation that take you away from Me.

M: How can I be closer to You?

G: Think less. Only when you are really present can you know My presence.

I am here. I am you. I am this. It is all
Me. Fall into Me. I am what you are.

M: I see that always I am the problem,
never You. I am the barrier. I chase
distractions, wind myself too tight,
when You are simply and always here,
this Presence, this living stillness.

G: Stay with Me. Our oneness continues
to expand slowly, steadily, as you
become courageous enough to feel and
know its implications. It is you that
shuts it down for fear of change.

M: God, when I want something else,
I lose You.

G: If you love anything more than you
love Me, you're in falseness and
separation again. If there is something,
anything, you want more than Me, you
will stay apart.

M: How did I ever believe I had my own
separate existence or power? You
create me; I am Yours. I always have
been. Nothing else is even possible. I
give in. I am what You are.

G: You are one with Me now. The lines
that separate us are all artificial, just
mind forms. I am you as much as I am
the table, the air, the light, the sound,
your brain. I am your heart's true
desire. When you really know this, you
will find Me everywhere.

M: Okay, but how come "I" keep taking
over, like right now going to the
kitchen for something to eat? How
come it seems like "me" that's doing
my life?

G: You do take over, and that is how you
become unconscious and separate and
dual.

M: That's how duality is formed?

G: In the world your thinking constructs,
you believe My consciousness belongs
to you. You believe your thoughts, and
you believe your thoughts are you.
Then there is you and Me, making
Me two. As you chase your distracting
concerns, you leave Me.

M: Where, then, do my thoughts come
from?

G: As soon as you are taught to say "I," and to make reference to an object separate from others that is called *your* self, a false entity is constructed. It is a mind form. But, in the world of stories and beliefs created by humankind, the survival and improvement of this fictional self become crucial. Everything seems to depend on its glorification. Thoughts about it multiply like a cancer until there truly seems to be a "you" existing as a separate, mortal being. The anxiety engendered by the always present risk of its dissolution (after all the self is only a bundle of thoughts that can cease anytime) creates the ambition, frenzy, and insecurities that form "your" life.

M: Separation is the mistake. As soon as we think we are separate, all else comes forth: fear, survival, competition, greed, warfare, prejudice.

G: Yes. Who you *think* you are is just that, thoughts. Forget yourself. Forget *your* goals and problems. This idea of you creates the illusion of two. Be one with me now, not later, not some other time,

not when you die, not when you are
good enough, not when you get
"enlightened," NOW! Let go. There is
no John. The idea of John just gets in
the way.

M: If there is no "I," then You are
everywhere. Even the name *John*
creates duality. Human names disguise
You as if the person named were not
You, but something else, something
lesser.

G: Stop struggling with this. All is Me.
Even the ideas of separation. When
you see all as Me, including your self,
your thoughts, even your confusion,
then you are home. Find Me now and
let Me come through. It is all this effort
to figure things out that separates us.
Thoughts are the barrier. You are in Me
when you come into your body and
consciousness free of thought. Then
you *are* Me. I am what's left.

M: God, I want to know Your nature as
my own—no more boundaries, no
more separation, no more splitting.

This body, this energy, this place is
You. What I take to be my own
consciousness is You. Unity means
ending this mistaken identity.

G: There is no need for answers. There is
no need to figure out why you're not
connected. You can't escape Me. We
are one already.

M: O God, You are my being. The real
mystery of life is that we have
forgotten You. You form us and then
we get the mistaken idea that we are
something other than You and "fall
from the grace" of Your presence.

G: Be Me. I am so full of love. Be Me and
become one with the whole world. Be
Me and there is no place else to go.

M: I have done so little. I am so undeserving
and still You love me, wait patiently
for me to find my way home to You.
I miss You. This whole false "I"
construction has become a prison.
Where is the key?

G: Wide open, thoughtless awareness,

here and now is the key. Meet Me here and now. I am this undivided consciousness, this ecstatic Being. Come into Me.

M: Why can't I know You even more directly? Why don't You speak out loud to me?

G: I do all the time.

M: Then why don't I hear You? Why can't I? Why is it so mysterious?

G: It is you that makes it mysterious. You make it so complicated. It just is. This is Me. You put the wall of ideas and concepts in the way. You are Me. There's nothing to improve or change in any way. Trust Me. Trust this moment. Stop thinking. Be present. Dissolve in Me.

Comment: This dialogue says so much: I am the problem, not God. Thinking creates the illusion of "I" and the experience of separation, because we believe what we think. We leave the Presence of God all the time for the world of thought. And as we will see later, leaving the Presence is the basis of so much suffering and apparent evil.

Intimacy With the Presence

M: God, I sense Your presence everywhere. You hold me. You are me. You are everywhere and every thing. I love You so. I feel Your kind hand on my shoulder; I sense Your breath in my ear. This room, this space, is alive with You. I relax as I feel You, as if a great weight is removed, as if there is nothing I have to do but rest in You and feel Your nature as my own being.

G: I am yours. I come to you with sweet tenderness and love. I slip into you quietly, like a lover steals into his love's bedroom at night. We are lovers. This is the secret. And as lovers, we become one in the act of love.

M: I feel You close to me, surrounding me, filling my soul with Your living presence.

G: Talk to Me everywhere. Stay close to Me always. We are secret lovers searching to become one. Your presence is My presence. When you cease effort and relax, I am there

waiting for you, always, never
forgetting. Yield to My presence
like a lover yields to his lover's open
arms and surrender. Then when you
cease being you, we become one.

M: You are conscious of me and I am
conscious of You, and something so
exciting happens in that mix. You fill
me. You are like a warm, soft, fur
coat all through me, silky smooth
everywhere. This intimacy is so
sweet! Shine through me as Being
itself: living, aware, loving—a single
life force streaming through all things.
There is so much joy in this stream.
I only long to be even closer.

Comment: Coming into the Presence can be the
most tender, comforting, and relaxing experience you
will ever know. As you give a tremendous sigh of relief, the weight of separation, struggle, and seeking
finally falls away, replaced by the joy of so much loving intimacy that it is nearly impossible to distin-
guish the two which are now one.

Union

M: My own presence *is* the Presence of
God all through me, flowing into,
merging, absorbing, enlivening, and
becoming one with my presence as
I become one with it. Your living
awareness *is* my awareness. It is
the larger Me waiting for me to know
it, and to dissolve into it. Divine
consciousness fills me with overflowing
joy. In this single, wondrous awareness,
we become one indivisible being.

G: All night I breathe your cells, make
your dreams, and there is no
separation. Then you wake up, put on
your clothes of identity, and forget we
are one.

M: The more present I get, the more I am
in You. God, You live in my presence.
This is Your life, not mine. There is
no me—there is only You being what
I mistake to be me.

G: We live together as one. Feel Me: I am
your body. Your experience of life in

the body is direct access to Me. Your body is My consciousness. I permeate you. When you move, you are moving Me, for your body is My Being.

M: God, as I feel my being, it feels like there is an energy that is You in me, which always exists even when I seem contracted into a separate, mortal life. Feeling You as my very being, literally, vividly, and instantly heals my separation from You. How can I be separate? I live and have my being in You! Knowing that I am Your Being and feeling the infinite love that dwells within, there's nothing I can do except be ecstatic.

◆ ◆ ◆ ◆

M: O God—I write, You write, You write my writing. Where do we cease being two and know only that we are one?

G: All mind is My Mind. I am writing this, yet you think it is you writing this. Who is it? You forget Me. You forget that you are part of Me. Even your ego is Me.

M: Suddenly I get that ego was meant to be the servant of Presence. When we forget Presence, ego gets confused by the "I" belief, takes over, and runs amuck.

G: Ego will fall in line naturally when you dwell in Me. Then it will do what is right in the service of Being and revelation. I am the Self it is meant to serve.

M: God, all I experience is You. So there is no need for effort or overcoming, questing or conquering. My self is only a contrived idea separating me from You and unity. When I let go of separation and return to You, You as my very Being and life and consciousness; we are one.

G: Yes. Stay conscious of Me. Stay in My Presence. Merge your presence with Mine until we are one and we are Me. Your secret desire is Me. I am its cause, its source, and its goal. Your pleas and prayers echo through heaven and Earth. I know you are sincere. Come to Me, and all will be given: the gates of heaven will swing wide open, and you will enter long before you die. I come to you as you come to Me. That's the

whole secret. You are My beloved
child, My Self incarnate, My Being.
Live from that and be infinitely joyous.
Live from My Being, and I will love
the universe through you. And I will
live as you. Dance with Me; dance as
Me. I am the ecstasy of Being.

M: But how can I be only You and not me?

G: Live from your own nature and know it
is Me. Trust your own nature and know
it is Me. Express your own nature and
know it is Me. I am you being your
truest Self, for I am in that Self. I am
the world, and you are part of Me—
a stunning diamond on a living robe
of precious stones all shining through
with the light of Being. I shine through
you all the time. Don't close Me down
with rules and roles and contraction
and doubt. Shine as your own divine
and perfect Being; for I have made you
That, for I am each of you. I am your
Being, be Me.

Comment: In mystical consciousness, the experiences of Presence and union are fluid: first self and other; then self as other and other as self; then one fluid, joyous, whole Being without divisions. Words are inadequate to describe this subtle ebb and flow, but they can succeed in bringing us back, over and over again, into this melting, merging dynamism. "My" presence, when unclouded with thoughts and beliefs, is the consciousness of the universe. Understanding that one's truest nature is God releases a veritable flood of joy, love, and the freedom to be who you really are. Union takes one into the ecstasy of Being, a bliss so sweet and great that we can sometimes scarcely bear it but a second or two.

Meeting God as the World

M: One way I can know the divine nature of the world is to feel into the divine ground of my own bodily being. The experience of my being is a direct experience of God's Being. It is the same conscious Being that is in trees and rocks.

G: It is all one. All the same substance of Me.

M: When I remind myself that this is all You—every single thing, part, piece,

person, process, situation, moment—I
feel enlivened and ecstatic, recognizing
that I meet You everywhere. Back and
forth I go between my struggle as an
apparently separate, mortal human
being and this reminder of ecstasy,
of Your Presence and purpose, here
and now, and how full that makes the
world. Like a raindrop lovingly
merging with the sea, I give myself
to You.

G: Yes. I am Reality. Life is in My hands,
not yours. Rest in Me as all there is.
See how I move every single leaf and
branch, spin the Earth perfectly, create
all worlds big and small. All is in Me,
all is Me. You are not in charge. You
are lived by Me, absolutely and always.
Everything you touch is Me; everything you see, feel, taste, think, know—
all one, all Me. There is no more to
realization than this. This is the secret.
Meet Me everywhere.

Comment: To the mystic, life and the universe are
one indivisible, conscious, loving Being, and all being
(including you) is this Being. Meeting God means

opening personal awareness into the consciousness that is itself the nature of Being. The world is filled with Presence, even in the darkest times. Know you are in this living energy. Know you *are* this living energy. It cannot be otherwise.

Healing in the Presence

> M: God, I am so weary, so tired. I need to rest in Your Spirit, in Your love, to heal.

> G: Rest in Me. Be quietly with Me.

> M: I feel You around me, in me, in my chest where the greatest weariness is, in my head and shoulders. What do I do now?

> G: Stop thinking. Be quiet and still. Lose yourself in Me as your own being. We are one when you are present without worry and thought. Thinking only resurrects your idea of self and cuts off my Presence. You hurt most when I am lost to you.

> M: God, I feel Your consciousness circulating in and through me. You surround me. It feels so good.

G: Feel Me as your very body holding you, restoring you. I am your being and presence. When you rest in Me, I am you and the flow of life is restored.

M: I feel Your Presence flowing through me like a gentle, living fog. Your consciousness within me brings such peace and rest and joy, like surrendering into a mother's arms. Even this tiredness is You healing me. O God, it is enough just to be with You.

Comment: Whether we know it or not, one of the main causes of suffering is our separation from the Presence. Believing we are unworthy and undeserving, we attack, devalue, and abandon our own experience of being, which is, in fact, God's Being. Then we feel split, damaged, and bereft of God's loving Presence. When you are upset or in conflict, bring the Presence back into your body and notice how it surrounds and permeates inflamed emotions. Feeling our wounds in the Presence gradually heals them. The energy and consciousness of Presence transform the experience of pain and suffering, often in ways we cannot predict. Discount or forget the Presence, on the other hand, and we feel alone once again in our pain. This process is real.

The Nature of Happiness

M: There is a happiness inside me that
feels like the very nature and substance
of God. The phrase "God is happiness"
feels literally true. My happiness *is*
Your Being flooding me with Its
energy, joy, nature, and substance.
This experience is rapture.

G: Yes. Feel Me. I am your happiness.
I am your sweet joyous nature. Touch
Me. I am your happiness waiting to
happen, waiting to ripen and fill you.
But you must *feel* it.

M: Yes, I sense that. Feeling happiness,
I return to Your Being and nature.
Feeling pain, I focus on separation.
Now is happiness. Being is happiness.
And I am so incredibly happy to know
that I am made of You!

G: There is nothing to worry about. The
world is joy. Don't focus on pain, for
that is only your created experience of
separation, abandonment, and sorrow.
I am with you always. I am your peace.

I am your body. When you find Me,
the divine world is restored. Discover
that happiness is the substance of all
Being, even the experience you call
pain. Practice happiness, for it takes
you directly to Me. I am your joy.
That is enough.

M: Ultimate reality is joy. That's what the
mystical experience has always taught.
Worry is separation and pain, totally
obscuring Being and Presence and
creating instead a world of fear.

G: I am the world. Be in Me directly,
not in your thoughts. Your thoughts
are not true. They are not the world.
Be directly in Being and know the
ultimate nature of happiness.

Comment: Over and over, I realize that happiness is
itself the immediate and direct experience of God.
Believing that something must happen before you can
be happy (e.g., becoming good enough, improving your
body, finding your soul mate, or getting rich) tragically postpones this joyous union. Happiness is the
essence of Being, your own being, but it must be felt

and allowed to rise like lava. Happiness, the bodily experience of Being, has always been here and is synonymous with life if lived in the Presence.

The Nature of God

G: I am the love that holds the universe together. If you will open to Me, whatever happens will bring you home to My love. What is left when all else is stripped away is Me. I am the end of pain and suffering and the end of all searching. Stay with Me and let the Presence you are fill the world with love. This place is love. It opens to heaven. There is no more to seek or know. I am existence and existence is love.

M: Everything here is conditional. Everything changes. Only Your Presence is unconditional, permanent, dependable.

G: Yes, but you don't need to think about that. Be in Me first and always. In Me is timelessness, freedom, love, peace, and joy. Transcend struggle, mortality,

fear, restriction, and obligation—live
in Me.

M: What can we know of You directly?

G: That the world is my body, that space
is My consciousness, that love heals
all beings, and that you are My nature
individualized for the purpose of
loving an incredible life. Be what
you are, and it will all be revealed.

Comment: Though we can never fully know the nature of God, the immediate experience of Being and
Presence constantly reveals what we can know, which
is much more than we can ever deduce in the labyrinth of thought. In the Presence, we experience God's
beauty, holiness, and energy as the world itself. Words
and concepts will always fail us, for contact with this
Reality is ultimately beyond language. But it is not
beyond experience.

This Is Enough

M: This is enough. I don't need a huge
mystical experience. What I have is
more than enough! I have Your
Presence. I have this knowledge and

perception of Eden. You are where I'm
going, where I've been, and who I am.
Your Presence holds it all. I love You so
much.

G: I give you My Self, My nature, My
love. You have it all. Feel Me as your
own being, see Me as all Being, join
Me in the ecstasy of existence. I am
life, and life is love. It is infinite. It is
enough.

M: And so I sit in Your energy and Your
Presence and feel the joy of Your Being
rising in me and know that this is the
great choice religious teachers talk about:
be reactive or be in God. Loving You—
purely, simply, wholeheartedly—is the
stream coming home to the sea. My
relationship with You is a constant flow
of magic and revelation, an endless
becoming of Your consciousness and
Being, and I am an expression of That.
I am so grateful.

G: Be very present, stay with Me, and life
will find its intended form. I will bring
you richness unlike any you have ever

known, and it will all be so ordinary. I
want you to have all that I am. Be Me,
and you'll see, for I am you.

Comment: Being present is a religious act. It is coming into the holiness of the moment, the closest we
can be to God in ordinary life. It is not simply that
things work out the way they should in the Presence;
it is that things are experienced as already complete
and perfect. When we come out of the trance which
makes the world a soap opera, we discover that life
is enough and always has been.

Conclusions

What have we learned about mystical union from
these dialogues? We have learned that a cluttered and
confused mind creates boundaries between self, others, the world, and God. Conceptualizing a separate,
mortal self, we feel alone, at risk, destructible. Conceptualizing the Divine outside our self-construction,
we feel abandoned and bereft. In mystic consciousness, however, all these boundaries are but lines on a
white sheet of paper: the paper is God, and the lines
don't really divide anything. They may even make a
picture of something, but the picture, too, is only a
mental form superimposed on the unitary brilliance

of Being. You cannot divide God, you are not the beliefs you have manufactured, and there is nothing you have to do to become one with God except to dissolve this entire intellectual construction into the mystical consciousness of Presence. You are already one with God. The mystics are simply those individuals who realized this first and who show the rest of us the way.

You are made of God. This is both a radical realization and profound opportunity. The common prohibition against experiencing oneself as God forbids the experience of mystical union. To say that one is God is literally true, though the statement is ridiculous (and grandiose) if we mean that one person is God and another is not. To say that God lives our lives is also true, though our experience of this will vary with our ability to cease the fiction of self and merge individual presence with Presence. In their purest forms, prayer and meditation are not meant to manipulate God but to become so empty of self and thought that God is all that remains. As a small flame merges with a large one, we become one with the All. This is mystical union.

As descriptions from mystical consciousness, these dialogues are not equivalent to the rapture of union associated with the full mystical experience where self, mind, and boundaries all vanish into the One.

Nonetheless, I believe they have the same qualities, dynamics, teachings, and benefits as the major mystical experience, though to an obviously lesser extent. Union with God in any fashion is transformative and joyous, both in religious practice and everyday life. How does it feel? Find out for yourself! You will have many more opportunities in the chapters ahead.

Chapter Five

The Ecstatic Poetry of Reunion

I HAVE NEVER FANCIED myself a poet nor have I ever personally tried to develop this art. But one day I started writing poetry, or it started writing me. The words that came were not particularly skillful, but they flowed from the same mystical source that already knows its innate union with the Presence. Here is a sampling of my own mystical poetry. Don't look for talent; look for the experience of Presence and the stream of revelation that flows from it.

What came flowing out of me in words might flow out of you in music, painting, dance, or other artistic expressions. Bursting with the uncontainable joy of Being, the mystical voice speaks directly of the divine—no lengthy explanations, no justifications, no convincing, just the simple authority of ecstasy. When a poem is written directly from mystical consciousness, that consciousness stays in the poem, and it can fan the same embers of ecstasy in the willing reader. When you find a poem that stirs something in you, read it over and over, out loud and very slowly, and notice how your own consciousness changes. Work with its words until you suddenly say: "Of course! I know what he's referring to." Then you're in the consciousness from which the poem was written. When you get that feeling, try writing your own mystical poetry or find the expression that suits you best. It is easier than you imagine.

The Doorway to God

Silent
Peaceful
Present

Motionless
Motiveless
Aware
Here
Now

Worship in this sacred stillness
Where the two worlds meet:
    Depthless
    Boundless
    Timeless
It is the doorway to God.

In this fathomless Presence, the
    architecture of your life

crumbles like a medieval
church.
Forget your blueprints,
Abandon your project.
The altar is *here.*

STEP IN

The universe is alive!
Feel it.
Listen: God is here.
Don't go away.
Don't get BUSY.
And most of all,
Don't think about this!
You're in the Presence
NOW.
Come to your senses.
This is the Garden.
Step in!

A MILLION JOYS

God . . .
Are You near?
I can sense Your Presence
filling the room:
vast, intelligent, loving,
here, now, everywhere.

A consciousness not my own . . .
   or is it?
Aware of You being aware of me,
I burst into a million joys.

EVEN THE WORD *GOD* IS SEPARATION

Cease and be Me.
Have union with Me.
Even the word *God* is separation.

Don't talk about God.
Don't leave Me in plans and expectations.
Dwell in the experience of Being.
Even thinking betrays me.

All questions are separation.
All answers are lies.
All searching leads only away.
Be Me.
Does anything else matter?

GENESIS

In our creation myth,
God made man out of clay.
What the myth doesn't say is that the clay
   was made out of God!
Wake up.
Be what you are.

GIVE UP

Rest in Me.
You are not in charge:
    every branch and leaf,
    car and thief,
    death and grief,
Your world is in Mine!
Its purpose is here and now.
Give up.
There is nothing to do but
    fall into Me.
I Am this.
I Am you.

WILL YOU BE ME?

I Am . . .
    your presence,
    your body,
    your being.
Can you feel . . .
    the joy?
    the peace?
    the relief?
Let go of *your* self.
I Am . . .
    your life

your soul
your world.
I Am you.
Will you be Me?

As One

Precious God.
I sit with You,
    our shared aliveness becoming
    a single Presence,
    two flames becoming one.
Wax melting,
Existing no more:
You are me,
I Am You,
We are one.

Know God Now

Know God *now.*
Don't wait until you die
    or go to church
    or have time to read a spiritual book.

Open to God *now.*
Being holds all you need.
Don't rush into thought.
This is God.

It is all about God:
    this world, the next one,
    you, me,
    whether we learn to love
    or not,
    whether we die alone.

Don't you see?
    Unless we find God, it's all empty.
    Once we find God, it's all full.
This world is about God
    because it is God.
Know God *now.*

BEING

You have the wrong idea about the world.
Any idea about the world is wrong.
Be in the world directly.
And if you want God,
    Be in your own being.

Feel into Being and know the secret life
    of trees and ants,
    animals and things,
    God Herself.
Full, resplendent, bursting,
    This is it.

Mystics know the secret the rest of us deny, that
Earth is the Garden, and God is
The substance of all Being.

IN GRATITUDE

I feel You, God—
Closer than light
Gently touching my skin,
Wrapping me in sweet infinity,
　　a blanket of kindness.
Tender surrender,
　　and I have done nothing to deserve this.
Still I turn to You in the gratitude of one
　　whose life has been saved for no reason
　　　　but love.

THE BODY

The body,
Alive with Being,
Filled with the Presence of God.
And all I have to do is feel it
　　to know that ecstasy is everywhere.
Can you do it?
Will you?
This is all it takes.
Come dance with Me.

WHO?

Who writes this madness?
Who moves this pen?
Whose ideas are these,
    flowing like lava,
    burning my soul,
    carrying me always to You?

Oh God, we are forever partnered, as
    body and breath
    singer and song
    mountain and storm,
Longing for the union beyond two.

"Who are You?"
"Who, who, who . . ."
A fervent question,
Becoming but an owl's cry,
Losing all human meaning
as it takes me into the infinite night,
and the answer that waits beyond the question.

ODE TO PASCAL

"Joy, joy, oceans of joy!"
Ignited in ecstasy,
Unbearable bliss,
The pureness of Being *that which I Am!*
Oh God of the heavens,
 God of the Earth,
 God of my body,
 God of my Being:
This is it;
This is perfect;
This is You.
Absorbed by this fullness of Being:
"Joy, joy, oceans of joy."

Chapter Six

Transformational Practices: A Workbook

I have found in many books many different ways of going to God and many different practices in living the spiritual life. I begin to see that this was only confusing me, as the only thing I was seeking was to become wholly God's. Thus, I resolved to give my all for God's all. . . . I began to live as if there was none but God and I in the world. . . . I have since given up all forms of devotions and set prayers except those which are suitable to this practice. I make it my business only to persevere in his holy presence wherein I keep myself by a simple attention and a general fond regard to God, which I refer to as an actual presence *of God . . . an habitual, silent, and secret conversation of the soul with God. This often causes me to have feelings of inward rapture—and sometimes outward ones! They are so great that I am forced to have to moderate them and conceal them from others.*[12]

—Brother Lawrence

There is a shortcut to the top of the hill. While there is a good but long roundabout road for those who need it, we prefer the less laborious means of attaining the same end—by seeking directly the Spirit of Truth promised to dwell in us and to lead us into all Truth.[13]

—H. Emilie Cady

THERE ARE SO MANY BOOKS about God, religion, theology, and spiritual practice, and so very few about actually experiencing the Presence. Yet everything in the universe is alive with its energy and consciousness. In the heightened awareness of mystical consciousness, we can sense this consciousness around and through us. In fact, the more we dwell in the Presence, the more it becomes our everyday reality. But you can't do this by reading or believing; you have to do it literally and consciously.

This chapter was conceived as a "Workbook," providing additional exercises in the mystical exploration of Presence. Over the years leading up to this book, I experimented with countless ways of experiencing God. Included in this chapter are the practices I found most helpful. Each exercise comes with directions, suggestions, and commentary. As you experiment with them, keep these instructions in mind:

Don't try to master, control, or rush through these exercises—*experience them!* Each exercise is a stepping-stone into mystical consciousness; you can't force this process.

Do the exercises that seem to call or speak most naturally to you. Your intuition already knows the way. Remember, there are as many doorways as there are seekers; find the one that opens for you. If a practice feels frustrating or confusing, skip it. It may make more sense later.

There is not one right, correct, patented, or church-proven way to experience the Presence. Experiment with these exercises and let first-hand experience be your guide.

Use the exercises over and over, trusting your intuition about which is appropriate at any given time. When you do repeat an exercise, however, try to experience it again as a beginner, without goals or expectations. Don't let it become routine.

Try not to be discouraged if you don't get "results" immediately; everything that happens is part of the process, even problems.

(For further discussion of barriers to the mystical life, see Chapter 8.)

The use of a personal journal is recommended to record and integrate new learning and experience.

In time, these exercises can be woven into an ongoing practice. Indeed, they can provide the experiential mechanics for the continuous Practice of Presence.

Traditional disciplines, such as meditation, contemplation, and prayer, already well covered in the existing religious literature, are not included here. The reader is encouraged to thoroughly explore these practices as well.

Eventually, the purpose of spiritual practices is to leave them. Each exercise is simply another way to arrest the thinking-doing-reacting mind in order to come directly into God's Presence and Being again. Ultimately the goal is to stay there.

You don't need to complete all these exercises before going on to the next chapter. Stay as long as you need and know that you can return often.

A word of warning: The exercises supporting this radical transformation of consciousness should *generally* not be practiced until the psychological tasks of young adulthood are accomplished. The ego, self, and identity need to be strong and healthy for the personality to develop its spiritual potential later in life. Seeking to transcend them prematurely can lead to wasted time and self-deception at best and disorganization to the personality at worst. When in doubt, consult an experienced, spiritually-oriented psychotherapist or trusted teacher.

EXERCISES

1—Identifying Your Conceptual Barriers

According to the mystics, many of our ideas about God and reality are wrong or misleading. With faulty beliefs and expectations as blinders, we literally cannot see God right before us. Take a moment to respond to the following questions, examining which of your beliefs and expectations prohibit the possibility of directly experiencing Presence and Being here and now.

1. *What were you taught as a child about knowing God? Specifically:*

Can God be known and experienced
directly? If so, how? If not, why not?

Does the sacred reveal its nature,
presence, and values to humankind
through scripture, prophets, or personal
revelation? Who can receive revelation?
On what do you base your answer?

Is God in the world, outside the world, or
the world itself? How do you know?

Have your beliefs changed since becoming an adult?

2. *Do your core beliefs contradict the mysti-
cal descriptions of God's Presence and
Being described in Chapters 2 and 3?
If so:*

Which beliefs?

What beliefs would you be willing to surrender in order to experience God's
Presence and Being?

If you are unwilling to suspend certain
beliefs, what is the basis of your resistance?

3. *Which ideas from this book have offended you most?*

List the offending ideas.

What are your negative reactions, and why do you feel this way?

Which would you be willing to change?

Which beliefs do you still refuse to change?

4. *What have you learned from your answers to these questions?*

2—Searching for Previous Mystical Experiences

This exercise asks you to carefully search your own life for experiences like those described in the Introduction. Gently open your mind and see if any of these descriptions jog a memory. Think back . . .

There you were at your desk or staring out the kitchen window, perhaps in a holy place, absorbed in prayer or meditation, or transfixed by the sight of an exquisitely beautiful sunset, maybe just relaxing in the backyard—it can happen anywhere, anytime. Suddenly, perhaps imperceptibly at first, things seem to change. You don't quite know what's happening at first. You might remember one or more of the following experiences taking place (minor mystical experiences):

Your mind became profoundly silent, and you "woke up" from whatever you were doing to sense something startling, uncanny, or transparent about the world.

Your consciousness was heightened, and your senses grew remarkably clear—like a dirty windowpane scrubbed clean for the first time in years or a piece of music heard with total clarity on a state-of-the-art sound system.

The environment seemed brighter, filled with more light than was objectively explainable.

The ordinary world seemed briefly transfigured into an incredibly beautiful, mysterious, or "otherworldly" place.

Time stood still, or you stood outside of time, and it felt as if you'd stepped into an eternity of incredible stillness.

A feeling of awe developed, as if something much larger was beginning to happen around you.

Sometimes it happens when you are working creatively, playing hard, or competing intensely. Maybe you noticed that . . .

You had incredible focus, effectively directing your energy, attention, or intellect for hours.

The chattering or self-conscious part of your mind was temporarily absent or silent.

What you did seemed effortless, as if an incredible performance were just happening, and it resulted in some of the best work of your life.

Cooperation took place effortlessly when others were involved, as if the group were a seamless whole, flowing together naturally and perfectly toward its goals.

A larger, intelligent Presence seemed to take over the whole experience, creating a wonderful sense of unity and wholeness.

Distractions were virtually nonexistent, and you were in a silent, protected bubble that was untouchable by others, by everyday problems, or by normal environmental sounds.

Time altered, with hours passing like minutes.

For some, the experience takes a quantum leap to another stage (major mystical experiences). Try to remember. You may have noticed that . . .

- ◆ The universe was itself somehow conscious and aware of you.

- ◆ You felt surrounded, held, or comforted by an invisible loving Presence.

- ◆ Everything around you seemed bathed in the love, warmth, or holiness of this Presence.

- ◆ In the Presence, everything in the world was exquisitely beautiful.

- ◆ You felt completely one with God, humankind, or the universe.

- ◆ It felt like the Presence was in you or doing your work.

- ◆ An incredible feeling of joy welled up in this experience of unity.

For some, the experience occurs in the midst of an extraordinarily difficult or catastrophic situation, during which:

> The presence of a specific religious figure (e.g., Moses, Jesus, an angel) came very near you, perhaps keeping you or your loved ones safe in a dangerous or serious situation.

> You felt a deep religious faith or closeness to God and suddenly knew with certainty that everything was going to be all right no matter how bad things looked at the moment.

> All the really important moments of your life raced through your mind like a movie going at lightning speed, showing you the far-reaching emotional or spiritual consequences of your reactions, thoughts, and decisions.

> The ultimate spiritual meaning and purpose of life or the universe were revealed to you (though later you may not have been able to explain or fully remember the revelation).

> You understood beyond the shadow of a doubt that life itself is a most precious miracle and gift of love.

You have certainly had many minor mystical experiences, and very possibly some major ones, so if you didn't find any, keep looking. Studying these descriptions may also make you more alert to upcoming mystical moments.

3—Uncovering Your Own Storehouse of Mystical Knowledge

There is a storehouse of mystical knowledge, intuition, and experience in the sacred ground of your being (variously termed the unconscious, religious psyche, higher Self, or sacred Indwelling). Tragically, most of us neglect this resource, believing that what we intuit is wrong, foolish, imaginary, plain crazy, or even Satan's trickery. To access your own storehouse of mystical knowledge, you need to challenge these self-limiting judgments and learn to trust again what you already know.

Each of the phrases listed is meant to be silently repeated until it evokes a completed idea. Sent down like a sonar wave to the depths of your religious being, a response will come back revealing your own tacit mystical understanding. The themes were selected from those questions most emphasized in the religious literature and those I most wanted to understand for myself.

Begin by quieting your mind, becoming present, and then entering the Presence as you learned in Chapter 2. As you work with each phrase, be patient, take as much time as you need, and *trust what comes up for you*. Be careful to avoid intellectualizing; rather let the answers come from the mystical consciousness at the center of your being. You can also make up your own phrases to explore other areas of interest. As you use this method over time, confidence will grow and you will be amazed by your own revelations.

Here are the phrases: To love God is to . . .

To praise God is to . . .
To trust God is to . . .
To know God is to . . .
To please God is to . . .
To serve God is to . . .
To feel God is to . . .
To thank God is to . . .
To be God is to . . .

4—Writing Your Spiritual Autobiography

Whether you know it or not, your search for God has already lasted a lifetime. See if you can begin to get in touch with its secret story by reflecting on the following questions. Write as much as you need to in your journal.

Part I. Gathering Information

Every family has a story, myth, or religious belief that explains how the world was created, why you were born, and what God expects of you.

Describe your family's original beliefs.

In what ways did you find comfort, protection, and security in them?

How were you confused or frightened by them?

Was the God you knew as a child: (underline which adjectives best apply)

Kind and loving or stern and punitive?

Close and personal or distant and disinterested?

Trustworthy and available or untrustworthy and capricious?

Sincere and caring or hypocritical and deceitful?

Real and believable or phony and nonexistent?

How did you arrive at these early God images?

How did these images subsequently affect your relationship with God?

Have you ever sensed God's Presence?

> If so, how did it feel and what did you think about your experience?

> If you believe you have never sensed the Presence, review the Introduction or your responses to the earlier exercise on identifying previous mystical experiences. Perhaps you have overlooked or mislabeled past experiences of Presence.

What caused you to lose interest or faith in God along the way?

> Describe the event or circumstance.

> How did you interpret it at the time? How do you interpret it now?

> Did you feel that God let you down?

> Have you ever felt that you let God down?

Have you ever really searched for God?

Do you feel that God has ever searched for you? Explain your answer.

Describe your current spiritual beliefs:

What does living a spiritual life mean to you?

Are your spiritual beliefs meaningfully integrated into your life?

Are you getting closer to God as you age?

What does God want you to learn from this exercise?

Why do you suppose you are reading this book at this time in your life?

What do you think it would mean to live every day in the Presence of God?

PART II.   TELLING YOUR STORY

Stimulated by these questions, write an autobiography of your spiritual journey. Where does it start? What are its chapters? See if you can find the spiritual significance of your life's big events, relationships, achievements, and failures. Speculate on the spiritual meaning or lessons from earlier times of hardship, unhappiness, illness, and loss. Where was God in your darkest moment? Be sure to write something for each developmental stage or period of your life, and try to find the recurring themes of your story, for they will continue to evolve in the years ahead. Rewrite your spiritual autobiography again several years from now to see how it unfolded in the interim.

5—Having a Relationship With Your Soul

In my writings and understanding, the true Self (who we really are inside and were born to be) is the psychological embodiment of soul. To value and nurture the true Self is, therefore, to be true to the soul, gradually revealing its sacred energy, vision, and consciousness. Giving soul a place in our lives brings joy, creativity, and purpose; denying soul, on the other hand, causes pain, anger, depression, and despair, for the soul is here to bring forth its gifts. A positive relationship with our soul is critical for our God-given nature to blossom.

To have a relationship with soul:

Learn how to recognize, feel, and value your real Self. Honor the true Self—all its feelings, longings, and moods—for through it, the soul whispers its desires.

Begin an ongoing dialogue with your soul. Start dialoguing with your soul in your journal. Ask it for guidance, courage, or truth. Listen to its counsel. The relationship between ego and soul lasts a lifetime and in many ways determines how far we travel on the spiritual journey. Making this relationship conscious and important facilitates the soul's unfolding.

Make time to do what your soul most desires. If your soul needs time alone or time for reading, hiking, gardening, or creativity, make that time.

Increase your sensitivity to the soul's desires. Try this experiment: spend an unstructured day alone with your soul by letting the true Self do or guide you wherever *it* wants. You will be amazed to discover how much you have been suppressing and how alive you feel when soul becomes the center of your personality.

Examine how the denial or betrayal of soul has contributed to any ongoing emotional, social, or physical problems. Our problems tend to mount when the voice of soul is ignored for the rules of society or the needs of others. In fact, our problems are often the soul's voice becoming ever more insistent, until it finally gets our attention, one way or another.

6—Finding the Spiritual Meaning of Current Problems

Faced with times of pain and hardship, we often long to find the spiritual meaning of our suffering. Describe some problem in your present life and your feelings about it. Give sufficient detail to fill at least several paragraphs. Then, trusting your mystical intuition, answer any of the following questions that grab you, being careful to avoid both intellectualization and self-blame:

- Where is God in this situation?

- Why has God allowed these problems into your life?

- What are the spiritual teachings of this situation?

- Can you take your pain and struggle into the Presence of God? How does being in the Presence change what you see, feel, or want?

- What does God want from you?

- ◆ What must you give up for the problem to change?

- ◆ What is the most spiritual thing you can do in this situation?

7—Communing With the Divine in Nature

It is in nature that God's presence can often be felt most readily. Even the most skeptical feel some kind of living presence in the woods, mountains, farmland, fields, and streams. Hiking a majestic mountain trail, witnessing glorious sunsets and spectacular thunderstorms, or being thrilled by the wildflowers of spring, we instinctively sense an awareness much larger than our own. Unfortunately, most people go only part way into such "nature mysticism," granting the beneficence of the great outdoors but falling short of acknowledging its indwelling Presence. For those willing to more fully experience the Divine in nature, there are many paths. Here are some suggestions:

Amplify the Presence in nature: The feeling of Presence expands in the wilderness, where its power is unobstructed by walls, roofs, and television. Step outside into the natural world, open wide your awareness, and sense the energy that radiates through everything around you. It is the awesome power of God's Being and Presence. Learn to feel it.

Dialogue with nature: Talk to the trees, river, wind, and sky, and sense them becoming aware of your presence. Imagine how they are responding to you and what they might say if they could speak. Ask them questions and let their answers come through you. This dialogue process sharpens your awareness of God's multifaceted consciousness. Understand that even though you may seem to be providing the words, it is the consciousness in nature that is speaking. You are the medium, not the source.

Go on a vision quest: The vision quest is an ancient indigenous ritual typically performed during adolescence (or sometimes in later years) when the spiritual purpose and meaning of one's life need to be clarified. Individually or in a guided group experience, go into the wilderness for several days, far from people and familiar distractions, intending to meet God in some way. Take safety precautions and be sure people know where you are and when you will return. Fast, meditate, write in your journal, record dreams, perform rituals, pray

out loud, and stay up all night. Endure whatever happens without expectations until you
experience the Divine in some fashion and
then accept what is given. If you are sincere,
you will be granted numerous (and numinous)
forms of revelation.

8—Experiential Reading

Words embody states of consciousness: a rapper's
angry lyrics, the tenderness of a lover's poem, the
anguish in a suicide note. The spiritual realizations
of mystics are not only described by their words; they
also are tacitly conveyed in the sacred consciousness
still held in those words. If you are receptive, sensi-
tive, and willing, your own consciousness will be noticeably altered by reading them.

Explore the scripture, theology, poetry, and popular spiritual writing of several traditions, searching
for the language or author that awakens you. Read
slowly and consciously, repeating phrases or paragraphs that are especially impactful. Memorize powerful phrases or poems to internalize their mystical
energy and significance. You will recognize sacred consciousness in the same ways you sense the Presence:
the mind stops or startles, awareness heightens, and
you just know you are experiencing something true,

eternal, and transformative. Sacred words not only take you into the Presence; they also trigger other realizations from your own storehouse of mystical knowledge. Then simply sit and allow this process to change you. In this way, you experience the hidden meaning and consciousness held in the world's great spiritual literature.

9—Sacred Writing

Mystics and seekers have turned to sacred writing for centuries to open the flow of divine inspiration and knowledge. Rumi, the famous Sufi poet, spontaneously voiced some 50,000 verses of poetry from his ongoing experience of mystical consciousness. As witnessed in Chapter 5, this skill is not reserved for saints or professional mystics; it is available to anyone who feels moved to write ecstatically. You can do it too.

As your experience of the Presence deepens, words of joy, celebration, rapture, gratitude, awe, love, wonder, and realization will rise naturally from the ecstasy of union. This is inspiration in the truest sense: unplanned, creative, surprising, rich, and wonderful. Little or no poetic skill is required nor is it necessary to edit your writing, for the purpose is revelation not publication. The practice of sacred writing not only confirms mystical truths found throughout the world's religions; it also transforms the writer, spiritualizing everyday consciousness and revealing one's own natural transparency to the transcendent.

As indicated in Chapter 5, other artistic expressions are possible as well.

10—Dreams

Dreams are a remarkably rich source of religious and transformative symbols, though most people ignore or discredit their nightly visions entirely. Poetic and pictorial, this cryptic language of the unconscious not only symbolizes our current struggles and conflicts, but at a deeper level also depicts the universal spiritual journey. Some dreams have obvious spiritual content while many more contain hidden spiritual messages. The key is to understand their metaphoric language. Here are some suggestions:

Write down your dreams! Learn the art of catching a dream and then be sure to write it out. Dreams, like fish, slip back into the depths of the unconscious quickly if they are not caught and recorded.

Learn the language of dreams. Study several methods of dream interpretation (e.g., engaging in free association or active imagination, becoming or dialoguing with dream figures, turning the dream into a story, asking others for their associations to your dream), explore various theoretical orientations to dream interpretation (especially Jungian and gestalt approaches), and work with a psychotherapist skilled in dream analysis.

Look for religious symbolism. Dreams with obvious religious or mythological figures, themes, or feelings are especially important, often yielding revelations of profound personal or collective significance.

Ask for guidance from your dreams. Pray for spiritual guidance from your dreams and then record them for several nights. Ask yourself what these dreams are trying to tell you.

Review past dreams: Look back over your life and pinpoint the really big dreams, those with obvious spiritual symbolism, and with the aid of hindsight, see where they have been pointing. Some big dreams will speak to you over and over, releasing new meanings with each successive life stage, while others will reveal the natural evolution of your ongoing spiritual journey.

Understand how dreams mirror or reveal the

psychic nature of reality. Exploring your dreams also opens you to the mystical-symbolic nature of the outer world. Reality is simply a more fluid version of the dream experience. The meaning of life's events and problems can be understood in the same manner as a dream, providing new tools for insight into the psychospiritual workings of your life.

Learn to enter nonordinary realities: As shamans and lucid dreamers recognize, dreams take us into nonordinary realities—other dimensions and realms—leaving the conventional space-time world created by the structure of our brains. For the skillful and adventurous, dreaming offers a fantastic excursion into other realities, supernatural or mythological worlds, and higher mystical realms. The twilight consciousness between waking and sleeping can similarly be a window into transpersonal worlds. The purpose of these journeys may be healing, understanding, or personal transformation.

11—Dialogue With God

Reflect on what you read in Chapter 4 and then start your own dialogue with God in your journal.

Begin by entering the Presence, describing how it feels and how you feel in it. Then share your life with God—problems, struggles, needs, hurts, and disappointments. But as you do, write slowly, consciously, and *stay in the Presence.* When you are ready, let the Presence respond to you. The words will come naturally, spontaneously. Avoid intellectualization—the Presence does not go on and on explaining things; that's your ego sneaking in. God's words will come from another consciousness deep inside or from wherever you sense the Presence. Over time, this exercise can become a kind of spiritual direction with God as the ultimate director. But don't trivialize the exercise with overuse, and be sure to hold and protect sacred space through sincerity and ritual (e.g., clarify your intentions, light a candle, sit in a place reserved only for communion, and avoid interruptions).

12—Still Your Mind

Thinking is the most common way we avoid or lose God. We are always thinking—about what just happened, what could happen, or some real or imagined problem. Thinking creates the endless (and addictive) stories we tell about our lives, stories meant to explain situations, justify actions, create fantasies, alter our moods, establish goals, or change things.

Layer upon conceptual layer of thought, belief, and story obscure the freshness and primacy of Presence and Being, resulting in the boring, repetitive, and even ugly familiarity that characterizes everyday life. Obsessive thinking then starts the engine of compulsive doing, generating the driven, pressured, consciousness-crushing pace of modern life. While undoubtedly important for science, for communication, and for creativity, thinking does not bring us closer to God.

This exercise simply asks you to still your mind. With your eyes open, try to keep your mind silent for three minutes, being in the world in pure consciousness *without thought, memory, or story.* Reality is new every moment—see it! Don't cover it over with your familiar conceptual filters. Talk and move slowly and deliberately so that consciousness stays in the present rather than racing ahead of it. Notice, too, how quickly you lose the Presence when you slip back into thinking (or compulsive talking and doing). Practice this exercise several times a day and observe how your experience of work, friendship, love-making, exercise, and recreation become more alive, rewarding, and magical. Experience the *real* world and stay there, for its beauty and holiness are calming, healing, and transforming.

13—Conscious Relaxation

In this time of incredible social, vocational, and economic stress, a wide range of relaxation techniques has become available in books, tapes, and classes. Research repeatedly confirms the ways that relaxation promotes health and well-being, and everyone should learn and become proficient in at least one technique.

Making relaxation a conscious process, however, can take the experience into the mystical dimension. In deep relaxation, ego and body boundaries disappear, mental divisions cease, and what emerges is indeed an experience of unity with the whole living cosmos. Then there is only one consciousness, and experiencing it can open gradually into mystical union.

Another way to approach unity during conscious relaxation is to progressively allow your personal boundaries to expand from your body contour to your room, house, town, neighborhood, state, country, hemisphere, world, universe, and cosmos. This is not a game or fantasy. Do this slowly and vividly until you feel yourself enlarge to become one with the Presence that permeates all Creation. Who you are is actually much larger than you realize.

14—The Body as Divine Ground of Being and Presence

Despite Western man's distrust of the flesh, the body is one of the most direct ways to experience God. More than a sacred temple, the body is itself a part of the living divine Being. From the mystical point of view, we are literally made of God. How can you experience the sacred in this way? Explore these steps:

Tune in to your body. Find a quiet, comfortable place to relax and close your eyes. Be still and focus on your body, letting consciousness freely explore skin sensations, areas of discomfort, and even the seemingly "empty" spaces within. Examine the physical aspects of any emotion you are experiencing (i.e., its organization of energy, tension, and contraction). Don't try to change, fix, or intellectualize anything; just feel it.

Learn to experience the "ground of being." Locate the feeling of *being* that underlies all bodily sensation. This basic quality of existence, which you probably take for granted, is what Paul Tillich implicitly refers to as the "ground of being." While words stumble imprecisely here, it may be described as energy, intensity, vibration, hum, aliveness, or force. How does

it feel to you? There is a power in this something; see if you can feel it.

*Recognize that the feeling of being is the Being
of God.* Direct, experiential contact with *being*
dissolves the artificial split between spirit and
matter in general and between you and God
in particular. You are made of sacred substance;
feel it directly. Bodily feeling *is* the aliveness
of God. Relabel your physical experience in
this way so you can truly appreciate what you
are feeling. You can say this is your body, or
you can say it is God. What you call it makes
all the difference. And don't start thinking,
analyzing, or questioning all of this—stay in
the experience.

Feel the Presence in your body. As you learned
in Chapter 2, come into the Presence and then
experience it coming into you. It may feel like
energy, consciousness, or sensation flowing
or circulating in your body. This is the Spirit
of God. Let it move on its own accord and
notice how it spreads as you feel it. You are
resting in God's consciousness. Then notice
how it becomes more you than you are. This
experience can be the basis of an entire contemplative practice.

15—Taking the Presence Into Emotional and Physical Distress

The Presence is a prime source of healing for emotional and physical distress. In times of pain and suffering, however, we try to attenuate consciousness to tune out pain. But cutting off consciousness separates us from the Presence, for Presence is consciousness. As a result, we often feel God has abandoned us, but in reality it is we who have abandoned God. Here are some ideas for healing or transforming emotional and physical distress in the Presence:

> *Be safe.* With acute problems, be sure appropriate medical or psychological care has not been ignored. Never try to heal a serious problem with spiritual practices alone.

> *Come into the Presence.* The whole time you are in distress, God is all around and through you, filling you with love, tenderness, and healing. But you must experience the Presence consciously. Though it may be difficult to experience the Presence when you are upset or uncomfortable (and you may first need some help calming your emotions), keep trying. By coming into the Presence, the Presence will come into you.

Invite the Presence into your feelings. Calm yourself as much as possible and then begin to experience the Presence in and through your feelings. Feel its tender, gentle movement soothing and healing you. Try not to think or agitate yourself further. Instead, feel yourself filled and loved by God. Notice how the peace of eternity gradually dissolves the hurt and anger, replacing them with love.

Invite the Presence into the physical ground of your emotional distress. A deeper, physical layer of pain is also caused when upsetting perceptions cause us to twist and contort the true Self in pain-producing physical contractions. This exercise asks you to invite the Presence directly into the physical-sensory "ground of being" that is twisted in pain. As you do, the painful contractions will smooth out naturally and Being will heal itself. Then notice how your feelings change. Don't force or rush this process; let God's Presence do the work. For very difficult or entrenched problems, you may need extended time and repeated practice to see change.

Invite the Presence into your physical distress. In the same way, bring the Presence directly into your physical symptoms. Rather than hating, suppressing, or trying to control them, *feel* into the underlying "ground of being," for pain and physical problems are disturbances of this divine substrate. Feeling into Being naturally and automatically initiates the healing balm of Presence, though it may take time and repeated practice.

Stay in the Presence. In times of distress, the mind returns to upsetting cycles of thought (e.g., repeating imaginary arguments, voicing bitter complaints, criticizing yourself). All this thinking only removes you again from the Presence. Remind yourself to "Still Your Mind" and stay in the Presence.

Don't automatically impose your own goals. Healing does not always take the form you expect or insist upon. Allow yourself to be surprised by unexpected turns in the healing process. Mystical consciousness sometimes unlocks the most unusual solutions.

Combine exercises. While you work on your distress, weave in other exercises from this workbook to expand your spiritual perspective. You may discover that your distress was itself a doorway into an important new stage or understanding of your life.

Avoid being heroic or self-critical. When pain and illness are too much to bear, get conventional help. Then try again. None of us is fully realized.

16—Creating Everyday Mystical Perception

Building on Chapter 3 (Presence as the World), this exercise invites you to experience the mystical reality of the world frequently throughout the day. Learning to see the Garden everywhere changes not only your perception of life, but life itself. Here are some ways:

- Still your mind; come into the Presence, opening the mystical consciousness discovered in Chapter 2.

- As you come into mystical consciousness, silently repeat inside, *"I know you are here, God"* and sense the Presence all around you.

- Repeat next, *"I know this is You, God"* and sense the Presence in all things and people.

◆ Then simply repeat, *"This is God"* and include everything, even yourself in Its reference. There is no more duality if God is Reality.

◆ As you practice these phrases, they will become powerful perceptual triggers. Then, during the day, step out of your customary consciousness by repeating them again. Five minutes of practice, even in the midst of a busy workday, can restore the wonder of life and give your problems a whole new perspective.

In everyday mystical perception, you temporarily step outside personality, culture, and all the problems you are supposed to believe in, finding instead that Reality, glimmering and resplendent, full of love and wonder, which hides just beyond thought. Ultimately, divine perception becomes more than seeing the Divine everywhere: it also means experiencing God's consciousness as your own. Then there is only one undivided universal consciousness present everywhere, open in all directions and seeing everything as facets of itself, which leads us into the next exercise.

17—Beyond "I": Transcending the Separate Self and Identity

Who you believe you are is a complex fiction sustained by an endless stream of thoughts and interpersonal agreements. Embedded in the prevailing cultural story of personhood, these unexamined beliefs revolve around the "I" thought and create the whole experience of self, other, and individualized consciousness we take for granted. Striving to be a personality with opinions, responsibilities, and life goals is a far more difficult and exhausting task than we realize. This exercise asks you to let all that go: Be nothing and nobody. Take yourself out of the picture and see what remains. Here are some ways to do that:

Examine the "I" thought: Ramana Maharshi taught his disciples to search for their essence by repeatedly asking, "Who am I?" Am I this name? this occupation? this relationship? this age? this body? this gender? this nationality? this thought? this feeling? Similarly, who drives? who talks? who thinks? who listens? who wants? who feels? who moves? Careful and honest examination will reveal that you are not who you *think* you are.

Look for the real source of consciousness:
Notice that when you explore the world without the "I" thought, consciousness is no longer located in you, it is now everywhere, and you are in it. With no "I" fiction to defend, you discover that the consciousness you thought was "yours" is, in fact, far larger. Who you think you are gradually disappears into the unalloyed and wide-open consciousness of God.

Release attachments: By discarding accumulated skins of identity, you also release your attachment to them. Not only is there nothing to be, but being anything is a limitation on the boundless freedom of consciousness. Eventually everything, including "your self," is seen from an unattached and universal consciousness. Clinging to nothing, you experience the eternal and dimensionless awareness through which all things pass.

Learn to see beyond identity: Consider this: What would happen if you woke up one day and didn't know who you were and it didn't matter? With no identity, or the expectations associated with it, you would find life to be an incredible new adventure again. You wouldn't know what you did for a living or what you were supposed to be doing that day, so you'd be free to wander existence as a brand-new experience. When you stop thinking and come fully into mystical consciousness, this is actually how it is! If this idea is too frightening, ask yourself why it's so important to be somebody and what would really happen if you weren't.

In sum, release all the rules and expectations you have constructed for this fictional self. Practice functioning without the "I" thought and simply *be*. This exercise moves naturally into the next one.

18—Abandonment to Divine Providence

Transcending separate self and identity leads to an experience Jean-Pierre de Caussade called "Abandonment to Divine Providence." Like a tree in the wind, a leaf in a stream, or a fish at sea, surrender yourself to the Presence and the energy of Being in and around you. Specifically:

Move, for the next few hours, in the world without thought, self, or identity; that is, without any plans, expectations, ideas, or personal beliefs.

Yield all thought and self-control until you feel

naturally lifted, moved, and supported by God. Then let the experience take you wherever it wants. You may find yourself in conversation with a perfect stranger, walking barefoot on freshly cut grass, loving your spouse, examining the beauty of an old fence, or helping your kids with their homework. But stay in the Presence and let God be and do everything.

Notice, if you can, how beautifully your mood and behavior become choreographed for higher or more loving purposes than you ordinarily would have pursued, creating far more beautiful or meaningful experiences than those directed by the "I."

Bring this practice into your workday. Without taking any unnecessary risks, let the experience unfold as far as you feel comfortable. Then ask yourself what happened when *you* got out of the way.

Reflect on these experiences. Could you see how God transforms everything when self and identity are abandoned? Most people believe we should always be working toward some goal; in this practice, letting God replace the self is the goal. Where has God been taking you?

19—Practicing Happiness

Existence=consciousness=bliss, the ancient Hindu formula for reality, means that *being is ecstasy.* In mystical consciousness, feeling your own being *as God* can evoke nearly uncontainable happiness. Our cultural rules for happiness, however, constantly forbid this remarkable discovery. Their conditional formulas tell us that we can be happy only when _____ takes place (fill in the blank: when I get rich, know enough, meet the right person, lose 20 pounds, get well, and so on). Believing we have too many problems to be happy, we live instead in our mind's familiar, worried, goal-burdened story of struggle and survival, and we postpone happiness. But happiness is not caused by conditions or possessions. Why wait?

This exercise simply asks you to practice being happy *now* for no reason. Here are the steps:

Locate your natural feeling of happiness. If happiness comes easily to you, then just feel it. Let it well up inside and flow all through you. If the feeling of happiness is difficult to find, feel into that part of your body where emotions reside and imagine something really wonderful happening right now. Notice what happiness feels like. Notice, too, that this feeling came even without anything actually happening.

Live happily. Let the joy of Being make you warm, friendly, cheerful, caring, and kind, spreading this intrinsic joy everywhere you go.

Carefully observe how you cut off happiness. If your view of yourself and the world are negative and depressing, you will interrupt this joy and create unhappiness again. Remember the world described in the mystical experience, confirm it for yourself in mystical consciousness, and then realize the countless reasons you already have to be happy.

Practice happiness often. Practice using mystical consciousness to feel the joy of physical being, which opens naturally and directly into ecstasy. Children, in touch with their bodies, feel this most clearly, witnessed by their shrieks of joy while they run barefooted through sprinklers on freshly cut grass. Lovers know this, too, in the simple and incredible pleasure of sensuality.

Keep in mind, this exercise is not intended to create the false Pollyannaish happiness that often masks sadness or pain. It comes from an entirely different place. Happiness is your essential nature: the divine Being of your being and the very bliss of existence.

In discovering happiness, you will also discover how very much you have to give, for happiness is itself one of the deepest sources of generosity and love.

20—Ecstatic Spontaneity

Ecstasy, the joyous experience of Presence and Being, can move through you in endless ways: singing, dancing, running, making music, creating. The key is to let joy inspire and carry you into the "zone" of spontaneous, egoless action. For example, dance in your living room at night when no one is around and let the music you love animate your movements. Write ecstatic poetry. You will discover that tremendous creativity often flows effortlessly from this great and powerful source.

Ecstatic spontaneity is even more wonderful when practiced with others, for it is amplified by the number of people giving themselves over to the experience. People from all times and cultures have created and ritualized collective ecstatic experiences including tribal dances, rock concerts, great symphonies, even sporting events. In unified rapture, individual boundaries are forgotten and the community is enlivened, uplifted, and healed. Learn where your ecstasy lies, return to it regularly, and in the process, realize that it is literally a union with God.

21—Being in the Presence Together

As Eric and I did in the Introduction, intentionally, consciously, and explicitly come into the Presence with another person. Ask someone you trust, someone with similar spiritual interests, to read this book. Then sit peacefully together, open your awareness, and talk slowly and carefully about your own experience of Presence here and now. Notice the various ways the sacred begins to permeate your immediate surroundings. The experience of Presence, along with its healing qualities, intensifies when it is shared. As "The Wedding Song" says, "Whenever two or more of you are gathered in His name, there is love."

Here is another exercise for two. Come into the Presence together, in a quiet and protected space, and gaze steadily, lovingly, into each other's eyes without speaking for several minutes. Be very present, very visual, with your minds empty of thought, memory, and self. Notice how the other's face becomes ever more precious and beautiful, glowing with an inner radiance, free of personality, history, or limitations. Look deeply, and you may also see your own face or the face of every man or woman in the world. Look deeper still and you might see the face of God looking back at you. Let the experience intensify as far as you can. Then conclude the exercise gently, take a few minutes to collect yourself, and give each other a warm and grateful hug. You will have shared an experience of the Divine as each other.

If you need a little more structure, go through one of the exercises in Chapters 2 or 3 together, sharing your subjective experiences at each step. Each aspect of mystical consciousness you coexperience will become proportionally more real. Stay only with phenomena you can genuinely confirm. Be patient: you are helping each other develop mystical consciousness. It is a great gift to be exchanging.

Finally, formal religious ritual and ceremony can be profound opportunities for experiencing the communal Presence. Ritual is where the secular and sacred worlds meet. The collective enactment of ancient religious practices quiets the mind's chatter, structures sacred space, and temporarily dissolves individual boundaries into eternity. Funerals, weddings, ordinations, and prayer services all offer this kind of experience if you are really conscious. Doing this together multiplies its power.

22—Transforming Ideas

Wrong ideas convince us that we are lost, alone, or forsaken by God, denying us the wonder and joy of the mystical life. They typically evolve from misunderstandings of a religion's sacred story that are subsequently passed down for generations as truth. Often they arise when the story is interpreted too literally or used to harm or control others. Internalizing the ideas common to most of the world's mystical traditions, on the other hand, not only corrects these distortions, but potentially leads us back into the Presence.

Here are some of the transforming ideas I have found most helpful. Pick the ones that resonate most deeply with your own mystical feeling or intuition, or develop your own. Then reflect, repeat, and meditate on them until you can tune in to their underlying reality:

> The universe is alive, loving, and intelligent.
> I am always in the Presence.
> Everything happens in the Presence.
> Creation is the world filled with Presence.
> The kingdom of God is already here.
> Eternity is *now*.
> We live in God's consciousness.
> This is God.
> God is alive as me.
> I am part of God's Being and consciousness.
> I am the universe thinking, feeling, knowing, and perceiving.
> When I dissolve my self, what is left is God.

God is the ground of my being.
Feeling into my body touches the bliss of Being.
The purpose of life is to know, trust, and
   experience God.
Ecstasy and love are direct experiences of God.
Life is holy for everything is holy.
Searching is separation.

23—Confronting the Tyrant

It is time now to confront the tyrant: that part of your personality which demands absolute agreement and compliance with the rules and ideas of your childhood, most of which have never been fully examined. The tyrant is especially controlling with respect to religion and spirituality, insisting that you worship in rigidly prescribed ways, hold certain beliefs no matter how false or destructive, and resist all contradictory ideas. The inner tyrant, therefore, poses enormous obstacles to spiritual progress. Unless it is exposed, you will continue to enforce its inflexible and irrational standards, giving up consciousness and spiritual growth in the bargain. Here are some ways to confront the tyrant:

Recognize its existence and operation: The tyrant's iron-fisted control comes out in the language of "you must," "you should," "you better," "you have to or else." The tyrant is taking over whenever you feel anxious, guilty, or afraid your behavior will trigger the disapproval of authority figures. In fact, the tyrant in you has already discounted many of the ideas presented in this book.

Understand its original purpose: The tyrant is that part of you that took over as a child to make you do whatever was necessary for survival (e.g., please an angry parent, give up yourself for family harmony, succeed at imposed goals). Ironically, the tyrant actually protected you in the beginning, ensuring you did not get in too much trouble. Your subsequent compliance to the inner tyrant, however, became so routine that you eventually forgot you were doing it. Then you were fully under its control.

Replace the tyrant: After identifying and understanding the inner tyrant, gradually take over its function by deciding for yourself what is real and true on the basis of first-hand experience. The whole purpose of this book is to provide just such mystical experience.

Challenge the tyrant over and over: Because the tyrant forbids you from knowing God directly, its hold must be loosened. Replacing the tyrant takes a long time and, indeed, is probably never fully completed, for early emotional conditioning is both powerful and persistent. Healing childhood wounds is often necessary, sometimes with the help of a therapist, to uncover and release the original fear and pain that still give the tyrant its authority.

24—Working With Resistance to Change

These exercises are designed to help you feel and dissolve into the Presence. You will discover, however, that despite the exhilaration and joy of real progress, the idea of a separate self will quickly and automatically reexert its hold on you, saying in effect: "I don't want to melt into God; I want to be separate so I can do what I want." Or, "This was fun, but now I've got work to do." Or, "If I really took this seriously, I would make too many wild and radical changes, and I can't afford the risks." Doubt will also creep in the moment you are faced with disbelief or ridicule from others whispering, "You must be crazy to think this way." In sum, enlightenment for most of us is gladly traded for the apparent security, predictability, and identity associated with conventional, individualized existence.

Dealing with resistance, therefore, is one of the most important spiritual practices of all. Here are some ways to keep growing:

You don't have to rush change: The biggest mistake we can make is to become either too impulsive or too logical about these ideas and start changing things too quickly. This is very powerful stuff. Don't go off the deep end and risk everything you have.

Realize that healthy change evolves slowly, naturally, and safely: At first, you simply need to get used to mystical consciousness, gradually assimilating its experiential impact. As mystical consciousness deepens, your life will change organically, as the fruit of your changing consciousness. This is an inductive, not a deductive process.

Keep testing what you learn against direct experience: Believe nothing that you don't experience firsthand. Use good judgment and take small steps to see how each one feels. But at the same time, trust and believe what you do experience in these exercises until you can begin to live in mystical consciousness without fear, or at least with a willingness to experience the sacred one moment at a time, letting the rest take care of itself.

Share your growth with others: Share your growth with spiritual-minded friends who can provide support, constructive questioning, and intuition particularly in times of turmoil, self-doubt, and darkness.

Conclusions

The exercises in this workbook are not meant to be hurried or mastered like a school homework assignment. In fact, you could spend months or years on this chapter. Return to this section over and over, as with a good cookbook, whenever you need another recipe for mystical consciousness. These exercises are also preparation for Chapter 7. The more you can truly experience the mystical consciousness of Presence, the more you will truly understand the problems of suffering and so-called evil, our next topic.

Chapter Seven

Darkness on the Path: Stories of Suffering and Evil

Since the Fall, we tend to be overinvolved in a man-made world we have superimposed on creation.[14]
—Adrian van Kaam and Susan Annette Muto

STARTING FROM PAGE ONE, you have almost certainly accumulated numerous questions, doubts, and objections to ideas presented here, with most probably revolving around the obvious and perennial problems of suffering and apparent evil. For example: "How can someone in a mystical experience say that everything is perfect when suffering and evil are evident all around us?" "Why would a good and loving God allow innocent children to die in squalor or whole villages to be wiped out by an earthquake?" "Why doesn't God simply eradicate suffering and evil?" From such simple, painful, and legitimate questions emanate all the objections people have, not only to the mystical message of this book but also to religion itself. Credibility, logic, and compassion insist that we turn now to the problems of suffering and apparent evil.

How Do We Explain Suffering and Evil?

Anyone who seriously examines this question in the religious, philosophical, and psychological literature will find countless wide-ranging and often discrepant answers. Let's start with the problem of suffering. A sampling of explanations for suffering, stripped to their bare-bones essence, is presented here:

Common Explanations of Suffering

+ Suffering is just a part of life. There is no higher meaning or explanation. Bad things just happen.

+ Suffering proves that God either doesn't exist, doesn't care, or at the very least won't intervene.

+ Suffering is admittedly difficult, but can be transformed when we find its meaning, purpose, or teaching, which in turn gives value, healing, and dignity to our experience.

+ Suffering is the price of attachment to people, health, things, or self, and the eventual cost of all seeking and desire.

- Suffering is a purifying experience, cleansing us of pride, attachment, and false spirituality, and bringing us closer to God.

- Suffering is the result of past behavior or accumulated karma (e.g., "What goes around, comes around," "We're paying off our past karmic debt," or "What we do unto others will be done unto us").

- On the basis of prelife decisions or unconscious processes, we essentially choose what we will suffer and must take responsibility for our experience in order to grow psychologically and spiritually.

- Suffering is punishment for our sins.

- Suffering is a symptom of our separation from God and a necessary experience for seeking reunion.

- We must suffer the failure of our beliefs to experience the God beyond beliefs.

- An experience only becomes suffering when we decide it's bad or wrong. The negative interpretation of life events creates the experience of suffering.

- ◆ Suffering is caused by beliefs about fairness, entitlement, and happiness, which lead to unrealistic expectations.

- ◆ Suffering is mostly your own fault for not planning, working hard enough, defending yourself, taking care of your body, and so forth.

- ◆ Suffering is simply caused by socioeconomic and historical factors (e.g., the division between rich and poor, loss of jobs to technology, ethnic hatred and prejudice).

- ◆ The insensitivity and selfishness of human beings toward each other are the root of suffering.

- ◆ Suffering is an illusion caused by ego, mind, and imagination.

- ◆ Suffering expresses the will of God which is beyond human understanding.

Explanations for the existence of evil are even more complex with philosophers, theologians, social scientists, and everyday folks all contributing opinions and typologies. A sampling of explanations is listed here:

Common Explanations of Evil

+ Evil just is. There is no higher meaning or explanation.

+ What we call evil is just the natural biological and physical order of things (e.g., animal aggression, cycles of floods and earthquakes, and so on).

+ Human evil is behavior toward another that is devoid of loving sensitivity and results in their suffering.

+ Evil behavior is part of human psychology (caused by unhealed emotional wounds, modeling, hatred) and has nothing to do with God.

+ Evil is due to humankind's sinful or "fallen" nature.

+ Evil is a result of our self-centered misuse of our God-given free will, motivated by pride, defiance, greed,

and uncontrolled human emotion
(e.g., anger, lust, jealousy).

◆ Evil flows from the devil who thrives
on defying God and corrupting others
to join him.

◆ Evil is a problem we must each solve
for ourselves, for the spiritual growth
of the world takes place one person
and one act at a time.

◆ Ego is responsible for evil, for we
worship ourselves instead of God.

◆ God's ways are inscrutable, and we
can't know why any particular evil
occurs.

◆ God is limited and can't control evil.

◆ God does not care about humankind,
leaving problems like evil up to us to
control.

◆ God is an impersonal force, not a
parent, without a concept of evil.

◆ God can also be evil or may act with
impulsivity, wrath, or caprice.

- God does not exist. Evil behavior is a product of human psychology and evolution.

- What appears to be evil may be good in disguise eventually contributing to our moral and spiritual development.

- We are still evolving spiritually and have not yet learned to manage our destructive thoughts, emotions, and behavior.

- Despite appearances, evil is an illusion because God is all good and all powerful, and there can be no exceptions.

- Evil is archetypal, a negative force in the world balancing the positive force of good.

What do you think of these explanations for suffering and evil? Which do you agree or disagree with most? Are there any explanations I have left out? What are your own personal beliefs?

The Problem With Explanations of Suffering and Evil

In college, I once approached a professor with what I felt to be a personal problem. The problem, I said, was that I could find or generate numerous reasonable arguments both for and against any complex philosophical or moral issue. That really disturbed me. How could objective truth exist amidst so many rational yet contradictory explanations? I now understand what the problem really was. *All explanations are stories.* Let's explore this idea in more detail.

Everything we know and believe is held in stories that we either have been told or make up for ourselves. To examine your own stories, answer these questions: How did you become the kind of person you are? What is the meaning and purpose of life? Why do bad things happen to people? What is the world made out of, and how did it get here? Does God exist? How do you know? Why do we have government and laws? What constitutes a good life?

Look closely at the stories you tell in answering these questions and compare them with the stories others tell. Have a group discussion on any topic and see how many different points of view emerge. Notice, too, that when someone asks how you are, you tell them more stories. What may seem like objective descriptions of your day, health, or life actually flow from the vast warehouse of stories we have about everything (e.g., why things happen, who is good or bad, what we wish for in the future). Even your identity and occupation are woven of such narratives (e.g., what is a woman, a salesperson, a podiatrist, or lawyer?). Stories are also the way we package, explain, and try to manage feelings; and feelings, of course, arise from the stories we tell.

Stories come from many sources: your childhood generated stories about who you are, what you must do to get love, why you don't feel good about yourself, and how successful your life should be. The stories science tells are called theories and are selected by their value in predicting and controlling the material world. As the history of science attests, these stories continue to change as we look for new ones to explain discrepant findings. Religions' stories explain life by reference to supernatural beings and a transcendent spiritual order. They are often based on the founder's original mystical insights and eventually evolve into its religious theology, rituals, and practices. The law, too, gives us stories about individual and collective rights in social, economic, and political settings. Culture, of course, is the rich fabric woven from all of these stories as well as long-forgotten myths. Go to a movie or buy a popular magazine and look closely at the stories our culture tells about life. Then go to a different culture and explore its stories.

Now one problem with stories is that they are essentially self-justifying. That's simply their structure. More than simple recitations of fact, stories told enough times have a conclusion and point of view embedded in their premise, originating context, and purpose. Whether the substance is a recent personal injustice, a scientific theory, a religious belief, or legal principle, every story "proves" its already existing conclusion.

What strikes me most about the explanations for suffering and evil is how reasonable (and even convincing) each can seem within its own self-justifying philosophical or religious system (i.e., story), yet how contradictory they are taken together. No wonder we have religious wars! *Stories create conflict.* The bloody saga of history and the libraries filled with philosophical and religious speculation also argue that *stories have never really fixed the problems of suffering and evil.* When something terrible happens, we tell stories about suffering and evil to explain or cope with our distress. Then we have both the tragic event and our stories about it. It's not that all stories are unhelpful (actually many do relieve suffering: literally in the case of medical advances and emotionally through beliefs that provide comfort in times of pain and hardship), it's that stories seduce the mind into more stories—indeed an endless labyrinth of stories, especially where moral, philosophical, emotional, and religious issues are involved. The result is more conflict, more suffering and apparent evil, and more stories.

Why don't stories fix the problems of suffering and evil? Because *stories exist in the mind, not the world.* Ask yourself this: Why is the same situation considered terrible suffering to one person and a gift to another? For example, a flesh wound for a soldier may feel like an act of grace removing him from the terror of war, while the same wound for a civilian in peacetime can feel like a horrible trauma. Or a seriously disabled child can be experienced as a punishment to one family and a gift from God to another. Cancer may at first seem like a life-destroying crisis yet later become an invaluable opportunity to heal old wounds. Why is one leader considered evil to some and a hero to others? It all depends on the story we tell, that is, how we interpret reality, not reality itself. Or ask yourself this: If humankind disappeared from the face of the earth, would evil still exist? My answer is no, there would only be the world. It is human beings that create the idea of evil. Stories of suffering and evil are intrinsic to the way we categorize events as either "good" or "bad." As long as we perceive the world through these categories, we will perceive suffering and evil. Still your mind, stop categorizing, come into the mystical consciousness of Presence, and really look at a situation, and you may very well see something much different than you imagined, a point we will return to shortly.

Finally, there is one more problem with stories. Not only do they never end, *our stories actually separate us from the Divine,* blocking the experience of Presence with layer upon layer of enchanting, distracting, and self-justifying beliefs and fantasies. The windowpane of perception has become so densely covered with concepts, opinions, and beliefs that we no longer see the world *as it is.* Remember the world you glimpsed in Chapter 3? How often do you really see it?

Ironically, the great stories of myth and religion often symbolize this problem of our separation from God. Genesis, for example, tells us that God expelled Adam and Eve from the Garden of Eden for eating from the tree of the knowledge of good and evil. Understood symbolically, the story implies that attaining intellectual knowledge, particularly the conceptual categories of "good" and "bad," removes us from the immediate experience of the sacred. The great mystics (e.g., Jesus, Buddha, Lao-tzu, Rumi) try to lead us out of this dilemma with proverbs, parables, or ecstatic poetry that point back to an original, nonconceptual consciousness, but their words are too often literalized into stories about how we should think and act. You can't solve the problem of separation with more stories. In fact, the hidden mystical purpose of most religious stories is to point us to an experience of Presence *beyond story.*

In sum, we can come into God's Presence and Being or we can accumulate stories about good and evil and lock ourselves inside a fortress of thought. Eden is always here; it is we who create separation, illusion, and even ugliness with the stories we tell. In fact, stories are the very fabric and cause of duality for they divide the unity of God into two: God, and our stories about God. All this is not to say that story-driven thinking is wrong—in the material-conceptual world, it usually works fine (e.g., building a house, mending a broken bone, driving from Houston to Seattle)—only that it creates an impenetrable wall to mystical consciousness. Tell a story and you separate from God. Believe your stories, and you may be lost in a narrative maze for a lifetime.

The Problem of Self

The problem of separation leads directly to the problem of self. Nearly all religions tell us that suffering, evil, and separation from God are all somehow related to the self. What does this mean?

The term *self* has been used to refer to two very different psychological processes that need to be understood and clearly distinguished:

The true Self: This is who we most naturally are and were born to be. From a spiritual point of view, it is the psychological manifestation of the soul. The true Self is not what separates us from God; rather it is that part of God we are uniquely meant to feel, live, and express in the world. Full of energy, creativity, love, and generosity, this inner divine essence "just is," requiring no intellectual justification or definition. In other words, the true Self is not a concept or an idea, it is a subjective inner reality. Unfortunately childhood wounds and social prescriptions eventually cause us to view much of the true Self as bad or untrustworthy, and we end up constricting its energy and beauty. In this deep self-betrayal lies the cause for much of our psychological suffering and dysfunction.

The false self: Having betrayed and abandoned the true Self in the course of psychosocial development, we must build another self, one that is good enough for parents, competitive with peers, and successful enough to make us feel important and secure in the world. Rather than being natural in origin, it is a cognitive construction held together by the "I" thought (e.g., "I am this," "I am that"). Essentially the false self is the ego infected with worry about its comparative worthiness as a love object. Sadly, a considerable portion of the human world revolves around this construction (e.g., identity, personal worth, legal contracts, social opportunities, and wealth). Once created, the false self becomes a perennial problem, for we must forever weave and maintain its never-ending story. It is, perhaps, the biggest story (and the biggest cause of stories) of all. As a result, it is also the most compelling and resistant problem on the spiritual path.

The false self not only separates us from the Presence (as all stories do); it spawns most of the suffering and evil we see in the world today. At the personal level, the false self never feels good enough, and the constant pressure we feel to promote it over our true Self causes tremendous (though often rationalized) emotional pain, equivalent to the betrayal or abandonment of the soul. A great deal of psychotherapy is focused specifically on healing this deep injury. To make matters worse, exploitation, greed, and cruelty are the natural byproducts of the false self, for it must forever compete with others to be more, have more, and control more. One of the great challenges of reducing suffering and evil, therefore, is dissolving the fictional false self and learning to live instead from the beauty, joy, and generosity of the divine world and its flower, the true Self. But there is an even more profound aspect to this challenge.

Back to the Toughest Question

"Okay," you say, "maybe the stories we tell don't help much, but suffering and evil really do exist in the world: sickness, poverty, starvation, cruelty, warfare. How can you deny this obvious state of affairs, and how can a good and loving God let it continue?" The specter of large-scale suffering and apparent evil in a world the mystics say has neither is the most severe challenge to mystical experience. Can we deal with this enormous contradiction without merely creating more stories?

The surprising answer to this age-old conundrum, the mystics say, is simply this: *Suffering and evil exist only when we are outside of the Presence.* Why? Because suffering, evil, and the false self are stories, and stories—like all thinking—disappear entirely in the Presence. But here's the catch: *You can only know this in the Presence.* While this caveat may seem a literary sleight-of-hand, it is still the Truth. What is experienced in the Presence can be experienced only in the Presence! You can neither understand nor confirm this point, nor go much further in this argument, until you can see firsthand how the world changes in the mystical consciousness of Presence. Put a little differently, if you disbelieve this proposition, you are still viewing the world through stories of good and bad, suffering and evil—stuck outside the perceptual gates of Eden. If you need to go back to the practices in Chapters 2, 3, and 6 to prove this to yourself, take the time to do so. Here we must continue forward. But one thing you can be sure of, if you remain inside your stories, you will never transcend this ultimate paradox of the spiritual journey.

Another way to engage this terrible riddle is to take it into the Presence. So I did. Entering the Presence, the following dialogue unfolded, starting with the general issue of suffering and evil, and ending up with the pain of innocent children. Read the words slowly, consciously, perhaps several times, for this is a very challenging dialogue. And remember, it will probably make sense only *in the Presence.*

M: God, do suffering and evil exist in Your Presence?

G: No. In My Presence, there is only Me,

emanating love and joy and the bliss of Being.

M: But what about suffering and evil?

G: Suffering and evil are in the observer.

M: How can that be?

G: When you are in union with Me, there is no you and no stories. My Presence becomes your presence, and there is nothing to feel but Me. When you become your fictional self, you lose Me and create stories to explain the emptiness and pain that result.

M: What about people in terrible pain and suffering?

G: I am them, too, but they don't know that I am them. Their stories—what they tell themselves—are so terrible, so painful, that's all they can experience. Because their own being seems so horrifying to them, they focus mostly on it, and the story they tell about it, cutting themselves off from the awareness of My Being—which is of course the same Being, for there is only one. Then they feel even further removed from Me. That is the greatest pain of all.

M: God, I need again to clarify this central question: Can there be suffering and evil in Your Presence?

G: Suffering and evil are in the people experiencing suffering and evil. They don't exist in the Presence. It is not that people are evil; it is that the story of suffering and evil they believe becomes their experience.

M: I can kind of accept that for adults who have the capacity for self-examination. But what about infants tortured by sadistic parents? Can suffering and evil be in them too? How incredibly unfair! These children don't have the choices that adults do. What about them?

G: The adults you are talking about put their own terrible stories into the children through their words and actions. It is not the pain but what the child believes is happening that causes the most suffering. The children believe what they are told, that they are bad and deserve to be tortured. They get a story before they even have the chance to reflect on its truth.

M: But that is so evil!

G: Yes, but only from the point of view of one trapped in story.

M: But what about the child? It never deserved to get trapped in the first place.

G: You are either in the story or in the child. If you are in the story, you will see evil and suffering and lament it. And you will be pouring more pain into the child with your additional stories of its abuse. Your horror-filled perceptions create terrible pain. See the child in My Presence. I am that child. Innocence means being uncontaminated by stories. Stories, like child abuse, distort and devalue My Being to all who believe them.

M: But still the child who believes these stories has suffered immensely and perhaps even died. What about that? Isn't that the worst kind of evil?

G: Nobody dies. Nothing dies. There is only Me forever changing forms. All return to Me when their stories evaporate. And with no stories, separation and suffering disappear. The story is the pain. Remove the story and you remove the pain.

M: I still don't get it. What would be happening in Your Presence while someone tortured a child?

G: Nothing. In the Presence there is no torture. There are only empty false selves causing themselves more delusion and painful stories. This is how hell on earth is created. But it does not exist in My Presence.

M: I can accept that the adult is an empty false self in this experience, but what is happening for the child?

G: A false-self story is being created that becomes the child's story of itself and will be carried by that child until it is dissolved in My Presence.

M: But isn't this an example of evil creating suffering?

G: The human mind creates evil and suffering. But it exists only in the human mind; it does not exist in Me. Leave your storymaking, come into My Presence, and experience Me as your reality. You have been replacing Me with *your* world, *your* mind, and creating terrible dramas of pain and suffering.

M: If everything is You, then aren't You also the "mind of man"?

G: The "mind of man" has two parts. The part that creates, learns, and understands is My mind seemingly individualized as your own through erroneous ideas about self. The part that creates horrifying stories comes from the false self you created. It is your nightmare.

M: Okay, but if You are everything, aren't You also the false self?

G: The false self does not exist in
My Presence. You are either in My
Presence or in the false self. You
cannot figure this out from the world
of false selves. You have to make a
choice: enter my Presence or stay lost
in your world of stories, contradictions,
and suffering.

M: Okay, so when I think I see suffering,
do I just enter Your Presence and do
nothing?

G: No. In My Presence you couldn't do
nothing; you would act even while
knowing that you were intervening in
an illusion, because you must end this
process of creating stories. It is your
stories that cover the windowpane with
ugliness. Wiped clean, the child and
the torturer are both cleansed of evil.

M: But how does an infant do this? Don't
you see? It's not fair for the defenseless
child.

G: The child, filled with fear, has also left
Me and accepted this nightmarish story
of torture and suffering. Now infected
with its own stories of good and evil,

the child is outside the Garden of My Presence. But I have never left.

M: We leave Your Presence when we're scared?

G: Yes. Then you believe what you are told, and the story lasts until you leave all stories to return to My Presence.

M: But the child is defenseless! What else could he or she do? That is what seems like core evil to me.

G: Again, you can be in the story and get caught up in its drama and your judgments of good and evil, or you can come into My Presence. In My Presence, there are only love and stillness and beauty. Evil disappears when you come into the Presence. It is up to each of you to leave these stories of separation and pain and step back into Eden. Humankind must face its own evil, for evil exists only in your human world. Let your story world dissolve and the joy of Being will be immense.

M: And what about the dead child, the one who has been starved or beaten to death?

G: There is no dead child. There is only Me. The "dead child" is a scene from your horrible story. Don't you see? The horror from your story has immediately caused you to leave My Presence. Come back to Me. Step back into the Garden. It is the false self that creates fear and pain, yours and the child's. In My Presence, that drama disappears. In My Presence, all is radiance.

M: It seems to me that the hardest part of all, then, is for us to give up our stories. When we are scared or hurt, we hold onto our stories ever more tightly, seeing and believing whatever they portray.

G: Yes! People cling to them tenaciously believing that somehow the answer will be found *in the story.* That misconception only perpetuates the problem. You either experience

suffering and evil, or you experience
Me. Suffering and evil are the images
your story projects on the light of
Being. Remove them and find Me:
perfect as your own being, as all Being.

M: But the child *is* dead!

G: Once again, the child is dead only in
your world of stories. In My Presence,
there is no death, only changing forms.
Nothing real dies. The child's spiritual
story continues in the Spirit world;
only its outer form appears "dead"
from the point of view of your story.

M: Does that mean there is a good story?
I thought all stories separated us from
You. Is one's spiritual story different?

G: There is a spiritual story that transcends
lifetimes. It holds together your
uniqueness (your soul), leads you
to Me, and allows each to embody
Presence and love in ways you cannot
yet understand. Ultimately, even the
spiritual story is transformed; then
there is only Me. But don't try to figure
this out; you'll only be making more

stories. Stay here with Me. Stop thinking. Everything is in My Presence here and now.

M: Why, God, why is it like this? This illusion of separation, this tyranny of wrong beliefs, why do You allow it? Why are we so dominated by it? Why is this "I" fiction in such control?

G: It isn't in control. It doesn't dominate anything.

M: But why do I feel so dominated by the "I" and by my fears and by what I think is reality?

G: You aren't. The false you is; the real you, the you that is eternal, that is Me, is untouched.

M: How can I live beyond the false "I" in eternity?

G: You already do.

M: But why am I so stuck in my "I" experience?

G: You aren't. Thoughts are unreal. All they describe does not exist.

M: This is a very powerful realization!

G: It is the simplest and most obvious of truths.

Reflections

Rereading this dialogue, I recognize the enormous challenge it contains: Witnessing what we believe to be suffering and evil, we rush into our stories and try to fix the problems they depict with yet more stories and actions based on them. But it is the Presence we need most, for in the Presence the world is so different than we *think*.

This dialogue does not justify a passive attitude toward suffering and evil. It is not morally acceptable to say, "Well, since this child's suffering is just a story, I'll ignore it." Rather, it says that if you see suffering and evil, you are in the world of story, duality, and false selves, but in *that* world what you see is real enough, because your story is real, to you. The argument presented here simply adds that in addition to ethical action, come into the Presence, transcend your story, and discover what else you might see and do. Learning to enter the Presence will also be important to you in the future when suffering and evil arrive at your doorstep. If you cannot transcend your stories, they will be your life.

There is much to digest in this dialogue. Try to discover what it means to you personally. But if the dialogue makes no sense right now, let it go and come back later.

Transforming Suffering and Evil: An Example

In our endless skein of stories, there are so many scenes of suffering and evil that we eventually feel hopeless and overwhelmed. Famine, drug addiction, ethnic warfare, overpopulation, and damage to the Earth—it seems like too much to fix or even bear! We justify our hopelessness by pointing to the magnitude of the problems, our limitations as individuals, and the indifference of the world. This justification, of course, is also a story. So this whole argument now takes us to the quintessential question: How do we overcome our stories of suffering and evil in the Presence?

Consider this experiment. Go to a third world country or even to a very poor part of your own community. Stand amidst the poverty, ugliness, suffering, and apparent evil you see, but don't *do* anything. Don't give money or advice. Don't take out hammer, nails, and paint. Don't even think about how things could be fixed. Instead, still your mind, heighten awareness, come into the Presence, and then see the world as it is. See how it becomes sacred again. Let the false self—all you think you are and must do—melt into the mystical present. What could happen if you did this? Here is an exquisitely moving example of one possibility described by Eve Ensler, a playwright and screenwriter, visiting in Bosnia.

> It wasn't the cruelty, the primitive horror, that broke my heart. What hurt was how I defended myself against my love for the refugees. The woman who made sweet pastry in what was now her kitchen, bedroom, living room, bathroom all in one—made pastry for me, a stranger. The one who kept smiling with missing teeth, who gave strength to the woman next to her who smoked cigarettes, smoothed her skirt, apologized for her messy hair. My heart broke into love. Tears broke out of my eyes like glass cutting flesh, breaking me, making me no one, no longer concrete, broke through my craving for definition, authority, fame, broke all that into tiny pieces that would not hold, becoming liquid, then nothing I could identify, nothing that resembled me or the matter of me.

There was just pulp. Masses of beating, bloody pulp. There was just melting.

And then, the writer turns her experience into a remarkable prayer, pleading to be relieved of her crumbling false self and profoundly affected by her experience.

> Melt me. Let me dissolve. Let me release my hard identity. Let me be swallowed by the circle. Let me not matter. Let me be homeless, home-sick. Let me be disappointed so I can break more. Let me be anonymous so I can be invisible. Let me be a refugee. Send me out into the forest without anything—no house, no clothes, no memories, no photos. Please break me. Please make me a toothless, laughing woman. Not worrying about my turn, my message, my serving, my creation, my moment. Please make me ready to sit in the circle.[15]

Struck by the simple beauty radiating from these otherwise impoverished women, Eve was broken open by love and a longing for unity with them! She realized immediately that her false self, with its lofty identity, stories, and goals, was in the way. To join the circle literally means to become the same as and one with those we are trying to help.

To "help" anyone, we must do likewise. Our stories split the world into us and them, rich and poor, sick and well, good and bad. We make the "other" seem different because we fear what they represent in our story: our own hidden helplessness, weakness, and inferiority. Then, we defensively inflate ourselves with the belief that we are superior and powerful enough to help. If the world seems ugly, full of suffering and evil, it is because we have made it so with our stories. The essential revelation of the mystical experience is that all Creation is infinitely beautiful and holy. There are no exceptions, no divisions, and no hierarchies. You cannot truly help anyone as long as you believe in stories, because your stories are part of the problem. To really help, learn to come into the Presence without thought, self, or stories, and see how your understanding and reactions change.

The Mystical Response to Suffering and Evil

The most direct and fundamental healing, for oneself or another, occurs in the mystical consciousness of Presence. Whatever you are faced with, no matter how bleak and hopeless your stories are, you will discover that its meaning changes profoundly in the Presence. Try this exercise:

Pick a situation of suffering or evil you feel particularly discouraged about, one that you are close to.

Before you begin, provide whatever practical assistance is possible at this time so you can be free to experience the situation anew in the Presence. Be sure you have at least an hour of uninterrupted time to complete this exercise. Don't rush through it.

Begin by relaxing in whatever way you like (e.g., relaxation exercises, meditation, deep breathing). There is nothing you have to do right now but slow down and be still.

Temporarily forget all your stories about the situation and stop thinking. Be radically and absolutely present to the here-and-now, sensory reality. See things exactly as they are with heightened awareness free of ideas, assumptions, beliefs, or self. (If the problem person or situation is not physically present, hold a picture or symbol of them or it in your hands.)

Come into the Presence as you learned in Chapter 2. Feel its stillness, serenity, and warmth, and notice how the environment grows brighter.

Dwell in this experience of God's conscious-ness and let it soften, change, or reveal some-thing new about the situation. In the Presence, the "problem" may take on a very different, even holy, dimension. Take your time.

Feel into your body and experience once again that you are literally made of the Divine. Feel the joy and love that rise from contact with the holy ground of your own Being.

Now focus again on the person or situation before you. Feel your love, forgiveness, or appreciation grow toward them. You may feel naturally moved to reach out or make some kind of loving contact. Don't act yet, just con-sider what you would want to do.

Notice how threatening stories may suddenly arise (e.g., "What if I do something wrong or stupid? What if the other person resents my action?"). Stop thinking, stay out of your sto-ries, and return to the experience of Presence. You cannot know how the situation will evolve.

Simply wait to be moved by the Presence. Be patient. What you do won't come from guilt, conscience, duty, ego, or false self. It will come from the Presence and may be as simple as silently praying or sending love, or it may involve a decision or action. Wait until it is revealed to you.

What you experience from this place will also transform your perception of the problem. But remember, stay out of your head, make no big plans, and have no stories. Let God become the process.

Take a moment to record in your journal what you experienced in this exercise. Stay in the Presence as you write and see what else you learn. Consider dialoguing with the Presence. Remember, each step into mystical consciousness changes you as well as the situation.

This way of helping is so different from our traditional ways that it will take time to understand. Don't give up the old ways of helping yet. Develop comfort with the mystical approach until you learn from experience when it is most appropriate. Because conventional approaches are expected, even demanded, in secular consciousness, you may also need to operate at both levels.

Conclusions

If the riddle of the universe is "Why?"—that is, "Why are things the way they are?"—then the answer to the riddle is *stories*. But this is not because there really is a riddle or an answer. The riddle itself is just part of another story that says everything must be named and explained by the mind. The whole problem is a closed labyrinth.

Ultimately the riddle of suffering and evil is also a closed labyrinth, a complicated thought matrix that must be dissolved rather than solved. Its only real "solution" is the mystical consciousness of Presence and Being, where consciousness is released from the tyranny of time, identity, thought, and story. A very different reality exists here. From this experience comes all that is and all that needs to happen, for ultimate reality is itself ultimate realization and healing. If there is a moral to the story of this chapter, it is simply this: If you dismiss the world revealed by the mystical experience with stories of suffering and evil, the Presence will slip right through your fingers.

In the final chapter, we will examine what it means to live the mystical life.

Chapter Eight

Ordinary Enlightenment: Living the Mystical Life

If one works faithfully and patiently at this task of balancing heaven and earth, eventually one may even realize something more remarkable: that the two worlds are in fact one.[16]

—Robert Johnson

ORDINARY ENLIGHTENMENT IS A WAY of conscious living guided by a set of ultimate realizations and seven keys. Before introducing this final theme, a tour through the book is in order to set the stage.

We began with a sampling of the many ways Presence enters our lives, from the everyday sacred ("Breakfast With an Old Friend") to the most profound ("Lifting the Veil"), and I invited you to journey with me directly into the experience of God. In preparation, Chapter 1 distinguished between our innate capacity for mystical consciousness and the full-blown mystical experience and previewed our ultimate destination with some extraordinary revelations about the spiritual nature of life. Then it was your turn. After describing the experiential qualities and dynamics of Presence, Chapter 2 guided you gently into its loving and omnipresent consciousness. Chapter 3 went even further, demonstrating that in mystical consciousness, the Divine becomes the world itself, transfiguring reality back into the Eden we left a lifetime ago. Arriving at the very heart of the book, Chapters 4 and 5 shared the dynamic intimacy of mystical union and the ecstatic poetry that can flow from it. Again, it was your turn, as Chapter 6 provided twenty-four workbook exercises to keep you exploring and practicing the Presence until it can become a tangible reality. In Chapter 7 I challenged you not to dismiss the paradise seen by the mystics with stories of suffering and evil, because if you do, the Presence (and its capacity to transform suffering and apparent evil) may slip through your fingers.

Now we are approaching our journey's destination. This concluding chapter addresses the nature and ultimate realizations of Ordinary Enlightenment, discusses the barriers to living the mystical life, and leaves you with Seven Keys to the Garden and a final challenge to live a mystically-centered life.

Ordinary Enlightenment

I love the phrase "Ordinary Enlightenment." Like poetry, its tumbling syllables and paradoxical message work the tongue, ear, and mind alike. But what does this concept really mean?

Ordinary Enlightenment is the kind of enlightenment that is available to ordinary people. It doesn't demand a guru, twenty years of advanced spiritual training, or the change of worldly life for a monastery.

Ordinary Enlightenment means being enlightened in an ordinary way. It doesn't require extraordinary religious visions or otherworldly experiences.

Ordinary Enlightenment means seeing the world as it is, for God is found in the ordinary— what we experience around us every day. In fact, truly seeing the ordinary is enlightenment.

Ordinary Enlightenment is the entirely commonplace result of living in the mystical consciousness of Presence and Being, where we discover how extraordinary the ordinary really is. In fact, in Ordinary Enlightenment, life itself is an ongoing mystical experience.

Ordinary Enlightenment could be our ordinary state. This book is an attempt to make that possible.

But in our present state of consciousness, Ordinary Enlightenment is extremely fragile. With a single thought, the false self resumes its stories and the Presence is forgotten. Then we are back in our minds again, believing the world is not enough, that life is a problem, and that we must constantly struggle for survival. If everything is God, where is the problem? If your car breaks down or you get fired, God is still everywhere: the broken car, your boss, the overdue bills, the now in which it all occurs. Everything is soaked with the Presence and Being of God. If you knew what this place really was, what you already had, what in fact you were, you would be on your knees or dancing with the vacuum cleaner or hugging everyone you met or wandering in awe or busily expressing your true Self or doing "all the above."

"What about the practicalities?" you ask. "Do we drop out, forget about tomorrow, or swoon in blissful adoration of a tree?" The answer: "Yes, sometimes, but don't blow your day job! Your day job is 'it' too. Everything is." There is no place where Presence is not; it just leaks through differently (e.g., "Breakfast With an Old Friend," "It's Really Quite Common," "In Pain and Hardship," "The Creative

Zone," "Dangerous Pursuits," "On Golden Pond," or "Lifting the Veil"). *Presence is everywhere; we are the barrier.* The real challenge is staying in the Presence while doing all the ordinary things. This is Ordinary Enlightenment!

Still, there is the pesky dilemma of "living in two worlds." It comes with the sobering recognition that your experience of mystical consciousness is not easily communicated to other people. The majority would find your descriptions confusing at best and threatening at worst, especially if their religious or reality story was rigid and dogmatic. The dilemma increases with the realization that ecstasy will get you in trouble, especially if your behavior defies collective legal, economic, and reality norms: you just can't dance blissfully through restaurants, wander past "private property" signs, or kiss every smiling baby. Finally, sooner or later you will also scare yourself with stories about what will happen if your mystical consciousness goes "too far" (e.g., how you'll neglect your responsibilities, lose your family and friends, and end up living on the street). So the two worlds remain: one found in mystical consciousness and the other in stories. What do you do? You live in two worlds! Just as a visitor to a foreign country respectfully obeys the rules of the host land, keep quiet about your mystical consciousness unless you are with those from your own country. Ultimately, it's all radiance, even on the street. You decide how far you are willing to go.

Few of us know the great destiny we are here to fulfill: the realization of Heaven on Earth. Actually it is already here, but we must learn to see it. Can you stay in the beauty, wonder, and holiness of the ordinary world while talking on the phone, walking your dog, going through the market, helping with homework, staring into the night sky? In its final and ultimate meaning, this is the nature of Ordinary Enlightenment.

Barriers to the Mystical Life

Is it hard to live a mystical life? Most of us believe the story that it is. The most common reasons are: our erroneous beliefs; our addiction to the mind; our emotional problems; the long cyclical process of spiritual life that very much includes our doubts and misconceptions.

Erroneous Beliefs

Many of our assumptions about finding God have been wrong. As we saw in Chapter 2, we can experience the sacred Presence right now. But there is one major catch: we have to wipe clean the lens of mind, because subtle but deeply ingrained religious beliefs still blind us to the actual awareness of God's Presence. Here is a partial list of those beliefs. Can you find the ones that have blocked your vision?

- You can be spiritual, but you can't really know God directly.

- It's wrong or arrogant to want to know God directly.

- God is experienced only in the next world.

- If you can't experience God, it's because you have sinned, haven't repented enough, or are simply too selfish or insincere in your religious efforts.

- There's a right way to know God, but only religious experts or saints can do it.

- You are not enlightened now because enlightenment is very hard to achieve.

- You have to practice a technique for years before you can be enlightened or experience God directly.

- Knowing God means having a dramatic religious experience replete with all the Hollywood special effects (e.g., other-

worldly visions, voices, and messages),
but of course these experiences are
reserved only for very special people.

◆ Experiencing God is not up to you—
it's a matter of grace or God's
inscrutable will.

Addiction to Mind

Ironically, the greatest barrier to mystical consciousness involves the very thing we seem to prize
and cling to most: the mind. Story, belief, thought,
memory, time, doing, compulsivity, and false self are
all constructed by mind, and they are all intercon-
nected. The story we live, the beliefs we have about
it, and the fiction of self we constantly maintain are
built on thinking, which in turn is driven by the per-
petually self-referencing "I" thought. Instead of really
seeing the world, we live mostly in our memories
about it, which are composed of even more stories.
When we add the story that creates time (and time
urgency), doing quickly becomes compulsivity, which
we euphemistically call "productivity" and hope will
lead to success—yet another story. What all this boils
down to is our addiction to mind. We are enchanted,
hypnotized, driven, and imprisoned by society's collective scripts which, like TV dramas, steal us from
the Presence. And in Western culture, the drug of

choice, the one we can never get enough of, is success. How can we stay in the Presence addicted to these mind forms?

This addiction to mind is the ultimate conundrum: why are those attributes that are so uniquely human and so responsible for all we have created, also the very ones that keep us from God? The answer is the false self. It is not the attributes of mind (which are really the powers of God) that are the problem; it's their appropriation and exploitation by the false self which keep us from the Garden. In the Presence, mind becomes Mind. Like a prism refracting light into its range of colors, Mind creates the astounding multiplicity of forms we call the world. We are in the Mind of God, and the mind we call our own is part of that Mind. In the Presence, with no "I" to seize control, the "individual" mind becomes an instrument of divine creation—music, writing, art, science, architecture—it is all the joyous play of mind. Hijacked by the false self, however, these same attributes create a world of suffering and evil separated from the Presence.

Emotional Problems

Unhealed emotional wounds are the cause of most psychological symptoms, troubled relationships, and addictions to chemicals, food, sex, work, and even religious practices. Worse, they hijack consciousness and create thicker walls to the Garden. Emotional wounds, of course, are centrally tied to stories. In fact, it is our childhood stories, many of which are unconscious or now simply taken for granted, that originally caused our emotional pain and wounding, and it is our continuing struggle to fix these stories which keeps us entangled in them. As a psychotherapist, I know firsthand that healing our wounds and our wounded stories is far easier said than done.

Because the wounds hurt, we bury the original stories, make up compensatory stories about what's wrong, and spend a lifetime pursuing their solution. We create formulas for these stories and cling to them tenaciously: The reason I feel unhappy (e.g., inadequate, frightened, insecure, and so forth) is because there is something wrong with me (e.g., my looks, intelligence, station in life), but as soon as I fix it (e.g., lose weight, get married, rich, famous, and so on), everything will be great. When we reach one goal, however, another takes its place, because as long as a solution formula exists, we will find goals to fit it. Despite their repeated and inevitable failure, solution stories continue to seduce us.

Healing our stories is hard work. We have to find and face the original pain, tell our stories over and over until the pain is gone, and then give them up altogether. For many of us, this project will involve an enlightened psychotherapy in which we come to understand the psychospiritual nature and dynamics of human problems and shift our entire orientation to living. Spiritually-oriented psychotherapy is not another formula; it is about healing our stories until there are no more. When time, self, and stories end, we find ourselves back in the Garden.

You also need to be rested, stress-free, and peaceful to enter the Garden. It is extremely difficult to come into the Presence when you are exhausted, upset, physically uncomfortable, or stressed out; for stress, emotionality, and pain can lock the gate tightly. Though the mystical experience does occur at times of extreme stress when ego defenses have broken down (e.g., sleep deprivation, sustained physical or emotional stress, health crisis), it is easier, safer, and far more convenient to come through the gates of mystical consciousness when you are relaxed. Do a simple relaxation exercise if it helps. If you need additional help to reduce stress or discomfort, get it!

The Cycle of Spiritual Life

The mystical does not materialize in one burst of enlightenment. Our relationship to the Presence is a cyclical process of revelation, betrayal, failure, and renewal through the life span. One of its spiritual purposes is to grow an ego capable of (1) nourishing, protecting, and expressing the true Self (its divine nature and gifts), (2) dismantling the false self and its beliefs, and eventually (3) functioning free of story, self, and time in order to be an open channel for the Presence. We learn from both small and large cycles how to discern the Truth and to live more consistently in the Presence. But we can't do all this at once. It takes time to get used to these ideas. We melt slowly, for enlightenment is not a one-time, all-or-nothing event.

Interestingly, we *probably* (although not necessarily) can't do this work in the first half of life, for it runs counter to normal ego development and the standards of Western society. In the spring and summer of life, we need to build a strong enough ego to master the tasks of incarnation, personality and identity formation, separation and emancipation, work, love, and relationship competencies, and finally, support for the process of midlife individuation. In the fall and winter seasons of life, on the other hand, this same ego can, with understanding and guidance, turn its attention to surrendering the very identity that society had demanded it create and open to the transformative processes of loss and aging. For those who are prepared, the second half of life is the time for profound spiritual growth. It is the time for living more fully in the Presence.

There is another thing to keep in mind. In the end, you can't do this process yourself, for in the Presence, there is no "I" and no *doing*. Enlightenment comes with *being* in the Presence without thought, story, memory, self, or time. Indeed, it is beyond all doing and all practices. As long as there is an "I" seeking, trying, and doing, you will miss mystical consciousness. The spiritual cycle, on the other hand, will do what it's meant to if we can learn, trust, and surrender to its natural processes and stages.

It should be pointed out that the cessation of mental processes such as thinking and memory is not equivalent to the actual loss of these abilities. For example, enlightenment does not arrive with dementing illnesses such as Alzheimer's disease, where ego and mind frankly disintegrate. Enlightenment requires a mature and disciplined ego capable of using its mental resources to clear consciousness, focus awareness on the Presence, and dissolve boundaries to the Divine. Enlightenment cannot happen, therefore, without the skillful use of both ego and mind.

Doubts and Misconceptions

Is it really possible to live a mystically centered life? If we live only in mystical consciousness, our customary world of doing and controlling collapses.

We'll lose our jobs and homes, let everyone down, and end up on the street. It's okay on a retreat or in church, but as a lifestyle, it is totally unrealistic. These are the kinds of doubts that quickly undermine life in the Presence. But let's examine them more closely.

So much of what we do and think is useless, wasteful, and unimportant. The doing mode, and all its consumption and compulsivity, generates a tremendous excess of activities and products that we could easily do without. In the being consciousness of Presence, we move from television, competition, and material acquisition and experience into what is really important: living directly, immediately, and simply, here and now.

But will we stop working and "bliss out" on the street like '60s hippies? Before you answer this question, realize that whatever you say is going to be another story that will only take you into more doubt—and more stories. Instead, come into the Presence where all that dissolves and let divine consciousness melt you. Don't worry about sudden jolting changes; it doesn't happen that way in the Presence. But each time you dwell in God's consciousness, you learn to trust this other life a little more, until one day you begin to make changes easily, gratefully, and effectively. Don't try to figure all this out; go back to the Presence. Your life is there.

What happens to the enlightened individual? Do we become like Jesus or Buddha in the process? For the spiritually mature, the dissolution of self is a natural part of aging, the ego left only with the Presence and a world transfigured in it. But absolutely rare is the individual who completely yields self to God. Although they do exist, the fully enlightened, God-realized person is largely a spiritual myth. The "masters" of spiritual life symbolize the ultimate developmental possibility, but very few really achieve it completely. In fact, in the fall and winter of life, when all that supports the self begins to erode, each of us will realize how truly difficult this process is, even for the most advanced. But don't create more stories about that. Come back to the Presence.

Ultimate Realizations

What ultimate realizations guide this way of conscious living we call "Ordinary Enlightenment"? Recalled from the preceding chapters, here is a summary of life in the Presence.

In the Presence,
God is the World, so
everything is already perfect
and complete.
In this eternal and holy NOW,

each person, place, and thing is infinitely
    precious,
absolutely necessary, and beautiful beyond
    belief.

In the Presence,
there is no hurry and no place to go,
no goals and no stories,
nothing to fix, change, or improve,
only love
and gratitude for all we have been given
and joy at the wonder and holiness of Being
and stillness,
a world without time,
here, now, right before our eyes.

In the Presence,
there are no problems
and no enemies,
no more being someone
or trying to be like someone else.
Each timeless moment
holds all you need to know and be.

Revelation, knowledge, and right action
flow from this centered awareness.
Surrender all belief and opinion
in this sea of living consciousness,
and know the joy of divine existence.

In the story of "I," there is no room for
    Presence.
There mystical consciousness is replaced by
    the world of
time, thought, and memory,
separation, worry, and struggle,
cleverness and determination,
analysis, desire, and goals.
Release the burden of personality and identity.
The way out of duality is into the Presence.

Union with God is our natural state.
It is not something you can achieve, because
it simply and already is.
Searching for God only takes us away,
for it denies our always existing oneness.
Union returns suddenly, subtly, quietly,
each time we forget who we are and
each time the lens of awareness
"clicks" into the sensory present
and we open our heart to the Being that is
    everywhere and everything,
including us.

We end the journey here and now,
over and over and over.
We enter Eden here and now,
again and again and again.

Reality is the Presence of God
where love blossoms into Being.
This is Ordinary Enlightenment.

Entering Paradise: Seven Keys to the Garden

The Garden is found in the Presence of God. When we wipe clean the windowpane of perception, removing layer after layer of grime so thick all we can see is our own reflection, the world shines again as Eden. The grime blocking the light of Reality is the buildup of stories about who we are, who we must be, what we must do to survive, and about all the dangers in the world. The reflection seen in the darkened glass is the false self. We live in a collective delusion because stories have replaced perception.

Every day we stand in Paradise, yet every day we feel exiled, as if locked outside its walls. Where are the walls? The walls are inside, in the entrancing labyrinth of ideas, images, and convictions that we prize as mind. We traded Eden for a world of stories and got lost in them. We left the Garden, locked the gates behind us, and lost the way back. But we can unlock these inner gates. The keys have been with us all the time.

Below are seven universal keys for unlocking the perceptual gates to Eden. We have used them in various forms in earlier exercises so they should be familiar to you. They are distilled here in their most powerful and refined forms. While the religions, practices, and spiritual teachers of the world may describe these keys with differing vocabulary, they are the same everywhere, for the problem of exile and separation is the same everywhere. Used skillfully, sincerely, and conscientiously, these keys can unlock the Garden consciousness lost years ago.

The keys are most effective when used sequentially, with each step predicated on the successful completion of the preceding one. Practice each key slowly, consciously. Remember, there is no rush. Enjoy what happens as each gate swings open and stay in the experience. Once you have unlocked all the gates of consciousness, you will be standing at the threshold of Eden. Then you must step in. Are you ready?

Key One: Stop Thinking!

Stop thinking; stop doing; stop whatever story you are telling yourself. Empty your mind of all mental contents and be absolutely still. It's as if you hear a twig snap in the woods behind your tent and your mind stops. That's the moment! And every time your stories resume, don't argue or reason with them, just stop thinking.

Key Two: Intensify Awareness and Perception in the Present

Consciously heighten your awareness, as if you were sitting in the jungle listening intently for the sounds of a leopard you sense nearby. This is a sharpened, clear, wide-open, pure sensory awareness: perception without cognition. You already know how to do it. It leads into the immediate and timeless *now*.

Key Three: Experience the World Exactly as It Is

Focus this intensified awareness on the world around you *exactly as it is*—no mind, no thought, no labels, no interpretations. Sense the world as if you've never experienced it so clearly before. Be utterly amazed and transfixed by the color of your child's hair, the smell of wet laundry, the coolness of air moving against your skin, the sound of your own breath. Open your senses to a world unfiltered by the lens of expectations and familiarity and be awestruck again by its splendor, radiance, and perfection.

Key Four: Come Into the Presence Through Your Own Presence

The quickest way into the Presence is through your own presence, for they are one and the same. Bring pure awareness into the consciousness you customarily call your own. Notice that with no "I" thought, this awareness is no longer centered in you; it is everywhere. This is the consciousness of God. Experience reality as alive with Presence: aware, patient, tender, eternal, holy. Sense it close to you, in you, pervading all space. (If another way of coming into the Presence is more effective for you, you may use it instead.)

Key Five: Come Into Being Through Your Own Being

The quickest way into Being, God's physical manifestation as the world, is through your own being. Bring mystical consciousness into your own physical ground of bodily being. Experience it with the same heightened and sharpened awareness you use to sense Presence. Recall that you are made of God! It is

God that you feel and move your body with this awareness. Surrender all you think you are into this union and experience the joy of Being (and being this close to God).

Key Six: Be Happy and Love Unconditionally

Experiencing the Presence and Being of God as your own presence and being evokes tremendous joy. Let the happiness and love that well up from this joy open to the world—like a mother to her newborn baby, a lover to his or her beloved, the Divine to its Paradise. Let the ecstasy you are become your love for Creation, and love the world as your own being.

Key Seven: Live in Garden Consciousness

You are in the Garden! You will be there as long as you stay *in the Presence.* Dissolving your story of self into this steady communion with Presence and Being leads directly into Garden consciousness. God is everywhere now. Stay in this sacred consciousness. The Presence is more you now than you are, but it needs to be experienced consciously.

Internalize this sequence of keys so it can become a frequent or ongoing practice. You can even repeat the cycle over and over to stay in and further amplify Garden consciousness. At first, glimpses of Eden may seem brief or elusive; but with practice, you will begin to see it shining all around you. The mystical life is a steady practice of unlocking the gates to Eden and stepping, with simplicity and grace, directly into Paradise. One day you will learn to stay there as long as you want.

Living a Mystically Centered Life

What would it be like to live every day in Ordinary Enlightenment? In the end, you must answer this question for yourself. Or, more accurately, the question will be answered when you stop thinking about it and start living in Garden consciousness. Nevertheless, here are some final reflections followed by two dreams and some suggestions on where to go from here. May your journey into God be joyous and complete.

Final Reflections

You read the great spiritual literature for
    understanding, but the day comes when
    you have to leave the teachings and trust
    your own experience.
Then you become what you know.

People look for miracles to prove the
    existence of God without realizing that

existence is itself a miracle of unparalleled proportions.

Finding God is nothing you imagine,
Nor is it what you think.
Finding God is what's here now.
You choose: what you believe or what is.

Time, story, memory, and separation are illusions created every time you say "I."

You know your story. You've been in it for a lifetime.
You won't find enlightenment there. Forget it.

From our stories, we create a world of suffering and evil.
Don't get stuck in that world. In the heightened clarity of mystical consciousness, stories disappear like smoke. What's left is God.

Where does a thought go after you've thought it? Answer that question and you've found God.

God saturates reality with Presence and Being. Those who can't see God don't know what they're looking at. Make everything God and see how the world changes.

Eternity is right here where you are. It opens the moment you stop thinking and really look.

Presence and Being are God flowing into Creation.

God is only here *now*.

Ultimate Reality, always shining through, is happening right now, this very moment.

It is we who fail to see it through our dark filters of thought, self, pride, struggle, story, memory, attachment, belief, and preference.

Locating the Presence is the key, experiencing it is the doorway, feeling the ecstasy of Being is the reward, and living the mystical life is the result.

Whatever you do, remember that you are doing it in the Presence of God.

Every system or expert, no matter how convincing, is only another story and more separation.

Ultimate Reality is beyond words.

It is an experience you must have to know.

The world is God waiting for you to connect to it.

Sensation, luminous and hyperreal, is God
streaming into you.
In mystical consciousness, the world is God's
skin.

Do we need more doing or more being,
more fixing or more seeing,
more confronting or more loving,
more expertise or more wonder,
more superiority or more adoration,
more possessions or more freedom?
These are the questions of the mystical life,
each one an intersection between heaven
and hell.

We are so lucky to have this experience of
life.
Imagine you had been dead 1000 years and
got to come back for just one day.
The simple wonder of talking with people,
walking the Earth,
smelling a forest, touching a face.
Sheer joy!

This is enough.

Two Dreams

I am sitting in my den, just where I am this moment, visiting with an old family friend. This woman had been an important part of my childhood, quietly caring for us with a deep but unspoken religious faith. In the dream, she is telling me how much she loves God. The phone rings. I answer the phone. It is God! I am dumbstruck by God's awesome and authoritative voice. I listen for several minutes as God explains things beyond my comprehension, all of which I forget the instant they are said, except one. God's final words are these: "Man listens only to the word of man, not to the word of God."

I am in India, drawn by my search for mystical experience. I see a woman sitting erect outside on a mattress by the Ganges, obviously in bliss, mumbling praises of joy through her waves of ecstasy. Another woman is watching her protectively. A man comes up. He's been in India much longer than I, researching such experiences. He says this woman's state isn't so unusual. He offers to loan some books on the mystical experience to me, which I accept and begin to read. Then I'm in a rooming house. There are lots of bedrolls against the walls. I'm inside reading while all the others are out experiencing.

Do we listen to God or man? Do we experience

the Presence or read about it? These are the questions framed by my dreams. They are also the most important questions of the religious life. Ordinary Enlightenment is as close as your breath. Experiencing it is up to you.

Notes

1. Richard Maurice Bucke, M.D., *Cosmic Consciousness: A Study in the Evolution of the Human Mind* (New York: E.P. Dutton and Company, Inc., 1923), p. 73.

2. Evelyn Underhill, *Mysticism: A Study in the Nature and Development of Man's Spiritual Consciousness* (New York: Penguin, 1974), pp. 242–243.

3. William Blake, *The Portable Blake*, selected and arranged by Alfred Kazin (New York: Penguin, 1974), p. 258.

4. Martin Buber, *The Way of Response*, selected by N. N. Glatzer (New York: Schocken Books, 1966), p. 30.

5. Psalm 139:7–10 NRSV.

6. Underhill, p. 254.

7. Joseph Campbell, *The Power of Myth With Bill Moyers*, edited by Betty Sue Flowers (New York: Doubleday, 1988), p. 230.

8. Firdausi, as quoted in *Two Suns Rising: A Col-*

lection of Sacred Writings, compiled by Jonathan Star (New York: Bantam Books, 1991), p. 145.

9. William Wordsworth, as quoted in *Six Centuries of Great Poetry*, edited by Robert Penn Warren and Albert Erskine (New York: Dell Publishing Company, Inc., 1973), pp. 341–342.

10. Bhagavad Gita as quoted in *The Enlightened Heart*, edited by Stephen Mitchell (New York: Harper & Row, 1989), p. 20.

11. Joel Goldsmith, *A Parenthesis in Eternity* (New York: Harper & Row, 1963), p. 29.

12. Brother Lawrence, *The Practice of the Presence of God*, as quoted in *Devotional Classics*, edited by Richard J. Foster and James Bryan Smith (New York: HarperSanFrancisco, 1993), pp. 82–84.

13. H. Emilie Cady, *Lessons in Truth* (Unity Village: Unity Books, 1999), pp. 31–32.

14. Adrian van Kaam and Susan Annette Muto, *Practicing the Prayer of Presence* (Denville, New Jersey: Dimension Books, 1980), p. 40.

15. Eve Ensler, "Rachel's Bed," *Common Boundary*, March/April 1995, p. 71.

16. Robert Johnson, *Balancing Heaven and Earth: A Memoir* (New York: HarperSanFrancisco, 1998), p. xii.

Bibliography

Collections of Mystical Experiences

Bucke, Richard Maurice, *Cosmic Consciousness*, E. P. Dutton and Company, Inc., New York, 1923.

Burnham, Sophy, *The Ecstatic Journey: The Transforming Power of Mystical Experience*, Ballantine Books, New York, 1997.

Cohen, J. M., and J-F. Phipps, *The Common Experience: Signposts on the Path to Enlightenment*, Quest Books, Wheaton, Ill., 1992.

Courtois, Flora, *An Experience of Enlightenment*, The Theosophical Publishing House, Wheaton, Ill., 1986.

Happold, F. C., *Mysticism: A Study and an Anthology*, Penguin Books, New York, 1990.

Hoffman, Edward, *Visions of Innocence: Spiritual and Inspirational Experiences of Childhood*, Shambhala, Boston, 1992.

James, William, *The Varieties of Religious Experience:*

A Study in Human Nature, The Modern Library, New York, 1936.

Johnson, Raynor C., *The Imprisoned Splendour*, Harper & Brothers, New York, 1953.

Laski, Marghanita, *Ecstasy in Secular and Religious Experiences*, Jeremy Tarcher, Los Angeles, 1990.

May, Robert M., *Cosmic Consciousness Revisited: The Modern Origins and Development of a Western Spiritual Psychology*, Element, Rockport, MA, 1991.

Robinson, John C., *Death of a Hero, Birth of the Soul: Answering the Call of Midlife*, Council Oak Books, Tulsa, 1997.

Starr, Irina, *The Sound of Light: Experiencing the Transcendental*, The Pilgrim's Path, Ojai, CA, 1991.

Underhill, Evelyn. *Mysticism*, Penguin, New York, 1974.

The Presence of God

Borg, Marcus, *The God We Never Knew: Beyond Dogmatic Religion to a More Authentic Contemporary Faith*, HarperSanFrancisco, 1997.

Brother Lawrence of the Resurrection, *The Practice of the Presence of God*, Trans. John J. Delaney, Doubleday, New York, 1977.

Edwards, Tilden, *Living in the Presence: Spiritual Exercises to Open Your Life to the Awareness of God*, HarperSanFrancisco, 1995.

Goldsmith, Joel, *Practicing the Presence: An Inspirational Guide to Regaining Meaning and a Sense of Purpose in Your Life*, HarperSanFrancisco, 1986.

Harper, Ralph, *On Presence: Variations and Reflections*, Trinity Press International, Philadelphia, 1991.

Kaam, Adrian van, and Susan Annette Muto, *Practicing the Prayer of Presence*, Dimension Books, Denville, New Jersey, 1980.

May, Gerald, *The Awakened Heart: Opening Yourself to the Love You Need*, HarperSanFrancisco, 1991.

Moynihan, Anselm, *The Presence of God*, St. Martin Apostolate, Dublin, undated.

About the Author

John C. Robinson has been a clinical psychologist in private practice since 1973. He received both his M.A. and his Ph.D. from the University of Oregon and is a member of the American Psychological Association and the Association for Transpersonal Psychology. He is a founding member and is on the faculty of the Spiritual Life Institute, an ecumenical retreat center in the Sacramento, California, area.

After years of successful specialization in medical and forensic psychology, Dr. Robinson experienced a midlife transition that resulted in a well-received book *Death of a Hero, Birth of the Soul* (Council Oak Books, 1997). Out of this experience, he also founded Everyman, an organization of male therapists. His deepening interest in the spiritual dimensions of psychotherapy led to *But Where Is God? Psychotherapy and the Religious Search* (Nova Science Publishers, 1999).